Spelling Rules!

Janelle Ho and
Helen Pearson

NSW Edition

Name: ______________________________

Class: ______________________________

Contents

SLLURP

SLLURP summarises the spelling strategies that you can use to learn new words.

Say	Say the word carefully and slowly to yourself.
Listen	Listen to how each part of the word sounds in sequence.
Look	Look at the patterns of letters in the word and the shape of the word.
Understand	Understand rules, word meanings and word origins.
Remember	Remember all the similar words you can already spell and relate this knowledge to any new word.
Practise	Practise writing the word until it is firmly fixed in your long-term memory.

Spelling Rules! Student Book 6 (ISBN 9780655092636) © Janelle Ho, Helen Pearson

Scope and Sequence

UNIT	SKILL FOCUS: Letter patterns	Morphology	Etymology	Homophones/ Confusing words	Topic words	WORD LIST
1	ge, gi, gy, dge, j					genre, geometry, genealogy, gyrate, indulge, grudge, judgement, jubilant, jest, juvenile, junction, hijack, prejudice, adjacent, adjoining
2		-ion: adding to silent e, ve, lve, be				corruption, exhibition, exception, restriction, distinction, desperation, cooperation, alliteration, devastation, hallucination, deception, evolution, resolution, revolution, prescription
3		-ion: adding to ss, nd, de, t				possession, obsession, extension, suspension, expansion, corrosion, invasion, exclusion, collision, persuasion, provision, admission, submission, inversion, diversion
4	words ending in a vowel sound					flee, pursue, statue, venue, cocoa, mosquito, rodeo, eerie, simile, guarantee, refugee, committee, verandah, debut, alibi
5		suffixes		homographs: premier, cabinet, minister	government	government, parliament, cabinet, politician, minister, senator, representatives, governor, premier, opposition, president, election, democracy, monarchy, federal
6	REVISION					
7		syn-, sym-, co-, com-, con-, cor-, col-	*me* (dimension, immense, diameter, perimeter, thermometer, semester)			synthesise, idiosyncrasy, syndrome, sympathy, symbiotic, symmetry, coherent, cohesive, coincidence, coordinate, accommodate, commotion, compensate, correlate, collaborate
8			*optos, athlon, medeor*	homograph: coach	occupations	coach, pilot, lifeguard, locksmith, optician, treasurer, choreographer, courier, tutor, sculptor, surgeon, analyst, pharmacist, athlete, paramedic
9		-ity: adding to able, ible				durability, probability, acceptability, compatibility, predictability, variability, changeability, irritability, visibility, flexibility, vulnerability, accessibility, invincibility, eligibility, susceptibility
10		affixes: -logy			environment	environment, rainforest, pollution, greenhouse, climate, recycle, ozone, ecology, irrigation, conservation, deforestation, flora, fauna, sustainable, atmosphere
11		bio-, zoo-, anthropo-, geo-, -graphy	*terra*			biology, biography, autobiography, biodegradable, microbe, zoology, zoophobia, anthropology, philanthropy, anthropomorphism, geology, geography, terrace, terrain, terrestrial
12	REVISION					
13	ior, ian, iar	-ity	*sen*			prior, senior, superior, exterior, posterior, deteriorate, median, alliance, valiant, pliant, ruffian, peculiar, plagiarise, matriarch, diarrhoea
14			*spek, sequi*			telescope, periscope, aspect, suspect, auspicious, conspicuous, despise, despicable, spectacle, speculate, sequence, sequel, execute, prosecute, consecutive
15		-ous				wondrous, perilous, miraculous, Indigenous, cantankerous, ferocious, gregarious, rebellious, voracious, precarious, instantaneous, spontaneous, righteous, continuous, ambiguous
16			*nova, vox, notare, reminisci*			novel, novelty, novice, innovate, innovation, vocal, vocabulary, advocate, vociferous, invoke, provoke, notice, notify, annotate, reminisce
17		-ic			science	solution, toxic, method, experiment, acid, alkaline, temperature, evaporate, thermometer, theory, equipment, chemical, microscope, hypothesis, laboratory
18	REVISION					
19		-ation, -ition				definition, repetition, condemnation, alteration, interpretation, continuation, declaration, cancellation, inflammation, explanation, exclamation, variation, identification, notification, clarification
20	ary, ery, ory	-ary, -ery, -ory		stationery/ stationary		military, anniversary, solitary, documentary, contrary, crockery, confectionery, surgery, nursery, treachery, forgery, sensory, contradictory, category, exploratory
21		en-, ex-, pre-, pro-, post-		homograph: entrance		enclose, engorge, entangle, extricate, exhale, excavate, exorbitant, precede, prelude, precursor, procession, prologue, procrastinate, proportion, postscript
22			*phone, onyma, patheia, magnus*			symphony, phonetic, microphone, cacophony, synonym, antonym, pseudonym, anonymous, empathy, telepathy, majesty, majority, magnify, magnificent, magnanimous
23				homographs: organ, appendix	medicine	medicine, bacteria, virus, pregnant, fracture, organ, influenza, abdomen, intestine, capsule, appendix, vaccination, immunisation, pneumonia, stethoscope
24	REVISION					
25	cy	-cy, ob-				cyclone, cynical, cyberspace, urgency, accuracy, literacy, numeracy, privacy, pregnancy, diplomacy, adequacy, delicacy, obstinacy, buoyancy, legacy
26	double consonants					territory, graffiti, suppress, pallor, assassin, apparatus, millennium, succulent, eccentric, gimmick, dilemma, pinnacle, abbreviation, etiquette, intermittent
27		sub-, suc-, suf-, sup-, sur-				subconscious, sublime, submerge, subordinate, subside, substandard, subterranean, subtle, succinct, succumb, suffocate, suppose, supplement, surreptitious, suspend
28		multiple affixes				incomprehension, unmanageable, discontinued, ignorance, invisibility, irrational, immobile, immovable, noticeably, symmetrical, unintentionally, uncritically, reversible, illegibly, predestined
29		suffixes, plurals	non-English words		money	currency, exchange, pound, euro, rupiah, baht, allowance, financial, budget, discount, subsidy, purchase, expenditure, millionaire, treasury
30	REVISION					
31	sce, sci					ascend, descend, transcend, scenario, obscene, adolescent, fluorescent, iridescent, effervescent, miscellaneous, convalesce, scintillate, conscience, conscientious, resuscitate
32					odd-looking words	onomatopoeia, asphalt, amateur, havoc, jargon, anemone, flummox, sleuth, nuisance, naive, pizzazz, eclipse, impromptu, labyrinth, conundrum
33			non-English words			trek, snorkel, mammoth, deluxe, carnival, rampage, maestro, berserk, gruesome, cologne, abseil, souvenir, gourmet, silhouette, entrepreneur
34			*astro*		space and time	asteroid, astronaut, astronomy, comet, galaxy, meteor, orbit, dimension, futuristic, chronology, medieval, terrestrial, archaeologist, palaeontology, Renaissance
35	REVISION					

Note to Teachers and Parents

Spelling Rules!

Some students are natural spellers, but the vast majority of students need formal, systematic and sequential instruction about the way spelling works and the strategies they can use to become independent, confident spellers.

The *Spelling Rules!* program is based on sound linguistic and pedagogical theory. It is informed by research into how students of different ages acquire and apply spelling skills, and how those skills move from the working to the long-term memory. The program closely follows the NSW English Syllabus. NSW Syllabus references are provided in the two Teacher Resource Books. The program consists of seven Student Books that are fully supported by the Teacher Resource Books.

Each student book contains units of work, with each unit designed to be used over the course of a week. The content of each book follows the suggested instructional sequence in the NSW English Syllabus. Each unit simultaneously develops new skills and reinforces skills from previous units. Where appropriate, topic words from other syllabus areas are included. When spelling rules and tips are introduced, only known sounds and letter patterns are used so that students focus on one skill at a time. Regular revision units enable teachers to assess student progress and reinforce key rules and patterns from previous units.

Spelling knowledge

Learning to spell involves developing different kinds of spelling knowledge. In many cases, particularly in the upper grades, more than one kind of knowledge is called upon at a time. As they work through the activities in each *Spelling Rules!* unit, students will develop:

- **Kinaesthetic knowledge** – the physical feeling when saying different sounds and words, and when writing the shapes of letters and words
- **Phonological knowledge** – how a word sounds and the patterns of sounds in words
- **Visual knowledge** – how letters and words look and the visual patterns in words
- **Morphemic knowledge** – the meaning or function of words or parts of words
- **Etymological knowledge** – the origins and history of words and the effect this has on spelling patterns.

Icons used in Student Book 6

This icon highlights useful spelling rules. The rule is always introduced the first time students will need it to complete an activity. There is also a handy summary of important rules on page 80.

This icon tells students that a special clue or hint is provided for an activity. It may be a spelling, grammar or punctuation convention, or a definition of a useful term.

Spelling Rules! Student Book 6 (ISBN 9780655092636) © Janelle Ho, Helen Pearson

Student Book 6

Units of work

Student Book 6 contains 35 weekly units of work. See the **Scope and Sequence chart** on page 3 for more information. Each revision unit gives students an opportunity to self-assess.

Word lists

In *Student Book 6* each unit (except Revision) has a list of spelling words. The core words in the lists have been chosen to support the learning focus and strategies being taught in the unit.

Spelling lists enable a spelling element to be focused on, and provide sufficient examples to consolidate the teaching point. Topic words come from other curriculum areas, such as mathematics and social sciences. In addition, homophones and words that are easily confused with each other are explained and practised.

SLLURP

Each word list begins with a reminder for students to SLLURP. SLLURP summarises the strategies that will help spelling move from students' working memory to their long-term memory. These strategies are provided on page 2, for easy reference.

Unit at a glance

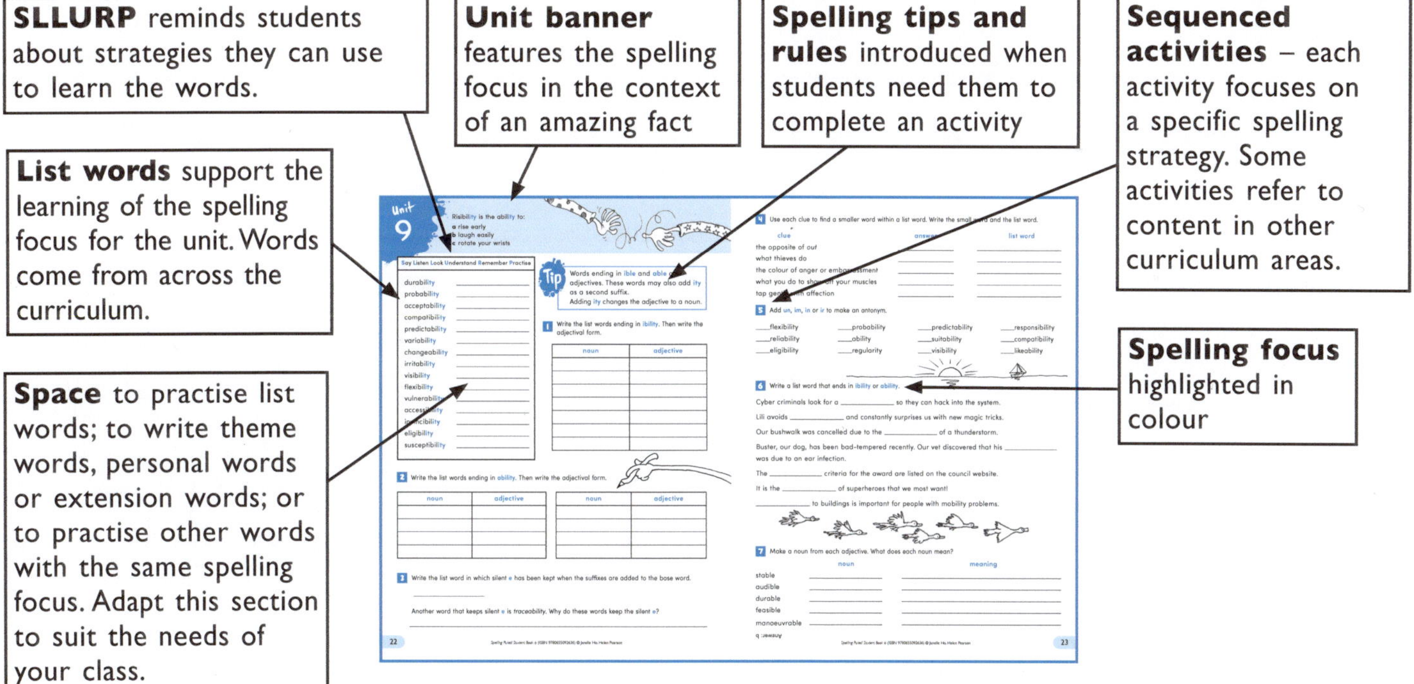

Spelling Rules! Teacher Resource Book 3–6

Full teacher support for *Student Book 6* is provided by *Spelling Rules! Teacher Resource Book 3–6*. Here you will find valuable background information about spelling development and spelling knowledge, along with practical resources, such as:

- teaching tips for every unit in *Student Book 6*
- extra word lists
- strategies for teaching spelling
- guidelines for assessment and diagnosis of errors
- activities to support struggling spellers
- worthwhile extension for more able spellers.

Unit 1

Julienne describes:

a the naming of a baby girl
b something cut into thin strips
c plans for a party in July

Say Listen Look Understand Remember Practise

genre ________
geometry ________
genealogy ________
gyrate ________
indulge ________
grudge ________
judgement ________
jubilant ________
jest ________
juvenile ________
junction ________
hijack ________
prejudice ________
adjacent ________
adjoining ________

Tip g usually has a soft sound when it is followed by **e**, **i** or **y**.

1 Circle the letter **g** if it has a soft sound.

gentle	energy	goalpost
gigantic	gymnasium	genius
ginger	gear	gallop
grudge	genealogy	giddy

2 Use some of the letters in each word to make new words with a hard **g** sound.

passenger ________
urgent ________
gyrate ________
pledge ________
genre ________
geometry ________

Tip Prefixes and suffixes are known as **affixes**.

3 Break each word into its base word and affix.

geometric = ________ + ________

jester = ________ + ________

adjoining = ____ + ________ + ________

disadvantage = ____ + ________

4 Use the list words as verbs, nouns and adjectives. You may need to add or delete an affix. Try not to use the same word more than once.

verbs	nouns	adjectives
to ________ a plane	the book's ________	a ________ champ
to ________ wildly	a traffic ________	an ________ room
to ________ in dessert	to hold a ________	a ________ pattern
to ________ harshly	treated with ________	a ________ animal

Spelling Rules! Student Book 6 (ISBN 9780655092636) © Janelle Ho, Helen Pearson

5 Write two list words that are synonyms. ____________________ ____________________

6 Complete the passage with words beginning with j.

In the Australian _______________ system, anybody accused of a crime is defended by a lawyer. In court, there is a _______________, who knows the law and controls what happens in the courtroom. A group of ordinary people called the _______________ makes the final decision about whether the defendant is guilty. If not guilty, the accused is free to leave. If guilty, the judge makes a _______________ about an appropriate punishment.

7 Write words with a j or soft g sound. The first letter is given.

The contents of the box are f_______________. Please carry it carefully.

Mum made an a_______________ to the length of my pyjamas so my little brother could wear them.

I am of a_______________ height, but my sister is tall for her age.

Karl longed to travel as a p_______________ on the Trans-Siberian railway.

My father has a cat a_______________. They make him sneeze.

I issued a c_______________ to replay the game because I wanted r_______________.

Dad tells us that holding a g_______________ can make one ill.

My grandparents tested their g_______________ and found that they have Dutch ancestors!

8 Which genre of books do you most like to read? Write a paragraph explaining why.

Answer: b

Unit 2

Fluctuation occurs when:

a fruit becomes rotten
b a flock of ducks flies in formation
c something changes constantly

Say Listen Look Understand Remember Practise	
corruption	________
exhibition	________
exception	________
restriction	________
distinction	________
desperation	________
cooperation	________
alliteration	________
devastation	________
hallucination	________
deception	________
evolution	________
resolution	________
revolution	________
prescription	________

1 Write the two list words that are different by only one letter.

________ ________

2 Complete the table.

verb	noun
attract	
	injection
	detection
exhibit	
exhaust	
	digestion
reject	
	direction
	infection
inspect	

Rule If the verb ends in silent **e**, drop the **e** before adding **ion**. *devote → devotion*

3 Write the noun form.

alliterate ________ separate ________ pollute ________ cooperate ________

4 Write the base word.

education ________ irrigation ________ hallucination ________

desperation ________ appreciation ________ devastation ________

Spelling Rules! Student Book 6 (ISBN 9780655092636) © Janelle Ho, Helen Pearson

If a word ends in **lve**, change **ve** to **ut** before adding **ion**.
dissolve → dissolution

5 Make a noun by adding **ion**.

evolve	resolve	solve	revolve
____________	____________	____________	____________

If the base word includes **scribe**, change **scribe** to **script** before adding **ion**.
describe → description

6 Complete the table. All the words follow the same pattern.

verb	noun
prescribe	
subscribe	
inscribe	
transcribe	

If the base word has the word element **ceive**, change **ceive** to **cept** before adding **ion**.
receive → reception

7 Complete the table. All the words follow the same pattern.

verb	noun
deceive	
	perception
	conception

8 Use the clue to make a new word that matches the definition.

word	clue	new word	definition
detection	change a letter	____________	gloominess
distinction	change 1st syllable	____________	end of a species
digestion	change 1st syllable	____________	build-up of traffic
revolution	change a letter	____________	conclusion

Answer: c

Unit 3

What does pretension mean?

a a claim that you deserve merit when you don't
b a number before ten
c preparing tent ropes

Say Listen Look Understand Remember Practise	
possession	______
obsession	______
extension	______
suspension	______
expansion	______
corrosion	______
invasion	______
exclusion	______
collision	______
persuasion	______
provision	______
admission	______
submission	______
inversion	______
diversion	______

Rule Some verbs add ion to make the noun.

1 Write the noun.

possess ______	impress ______
confess ______	discuss ______
concuss ______	obsess ______

impress...

2 Describe the pattern used in question 1.

______

______

Rule For some words ending in t, change t to ss before adding ion.
admit → *admission*
If a word ends in nd, change d to s before adding ion.
extend → *extension*

3 Write the noun.

permit ______ submit ______ omit ______
expand ______ suspend ______ comprehend ______

4 *Admit* has two related nouns: *admission* and *admittance*. Use a dictionary to find the meaning of each word. Use each word in a sentence.

admission ______

______

admittance ______

______

Spelling Rules! Student Book 6 (ISBN 9780655092636) © Janelle Ho, Helen Pearson

If the verb ends in **de**, drop the **e** and change **d** to **s** before adding **ion**.
divide → *division*

5 Write the noun form.

explode	collide	invade	exclude	persuade
______	______	______	______	______
conclude	include	erode	decide	evade
______	______	______	______	______

Tip

Some words are always used together. This is called **collocation**.
separation from not *separation with*
The underlined words are **prepositions**.

6 Write a list word and the preposition it goes with to complete each sentence.

The player's ______________ ______ the first team was due to injury.

The ______________ ______ the project deadline was greeted with cheers by the whole class.

Susie didn't have to say anything; her face was an ______________ ______ her guilt.

The shattered glass at the intersection was due to the ______________ ______ two cars earlier.

Mr King displays his ______________ ______ toy cars in his shed. It's full to the ceiling!

There was rust on the machine due to ______________ ______ the iron parts.

7 Rewrite each sentence using a list word. If you can, begin your sentence with the list word.

The scientist Charles Darwin proposed a theory of how living things have evolved.

____

This year I have resolved to talk to one new person a month.

____

The local council has finally said they will permit my parents to build a pool!

____

My prize-winning painting will be exhibited in the Town Hall next month.

____

Anyone caught writing graffiti on the walls will be suspended.

____

Answer: a

Unit 4

What is whangee?

a the opposite of a wedgie
b bamboo used for making canes
c someone who has made one hundred bungee jumps

Say Listen Look Understand Remember Practise

flee	______
pursue	______
statue	______
venue	______
cocoa	______
mosquito	______
rodeo	______
eerie	______
simile	______
guarantee	______
refugee	______
committee	______
verandah	______
debut	______
alibi	______

1 Write list words that end with these sounds.

long o as in toe ______ ______ ______

long e as in key ______ ______ ______ ______ ______ ______

long oo as in true ______ ______ ______ ______

2 Write a list word that has a silent letter.

______

3 Which list word is a homophone? Write each word and its meaning.

______ ______

______ ______

4 Write the plural.

verandah	mosquito	refugee	volcano	alibi
______	______	______	______	______

5 Write the language each word comes from and its meaning. Use a dictionary if you need help.

	language	meaning
cocoa	______	______
rodeo	______	______
verandah	______	______
debut	______	______
alibi	______	______

6 Most of the vowels have been left out of these sentences. Write each sentence correctly.

Ths nw cmptr gdgt cms wth a fr-yr grnte.

____

Th wnd whstlng thrgh th crck in th wndw mks n eri snd.

____

Do y knw th vnu fr th drss rhrsl?

____

Lins prsu thr pry in pcks t incrs thr chncs of mkng a kll.

____

Tip

A **simile** describes something by comparing it to something else.
It uses *like* or *as* to make the comparison.
The dancer flopped around like a fish out of water.
The dancer moved as gracefully as a swan.

7 Write similes using these words.

statue ____

cocoa ____

eerie ____

rodeo ____

mosquito ____

8 Write list words.

The local community hall will be a good ______________ for our meeting.

Hot ______________ can warm you up in winter.

The ______________ net around my bed has a hole in it, and I got bitten last night.

The light before the thunderstorm was ______________.

9 Write the correct form of the verb to complete each sentence.

The police ______________ the shoplifters and eventually caught them.
pursue

This gold pass ______________ you free entry to the movies for one year!
guarantee

Our cat Mimi ______________ into the house when the dogs started barking.
flee

Answer: b

Unit 5

A diarchy is:

a two arches in a row
b a human with two heads
c a State governed by two rulers

Say Listen Look Understand Remember Practise	
government	________
parliament	________
cabinet	________
politician	________
minister	________
senator	________
representatives	________
governor	________
premier	________
opposition	________
president	________
election	________
democracy	________
monarchy	________
federal	________

1 Break each word into its base word and suffix.

government = ________ + ________
election = ________ + ________
monarchy = ________ + ________
opposition = ________ + ________
politician = ________ + ________
president = ________ + ________
governor = ________ + ________

2 Look at the words in question 1.

Which words have the same base word?

________ ________

In which words does the base word change when the suffix is added?

________ ________
____

3 Write the list words that refer to people who work in government. Circle the word that is not a member of the Australian government.

________ ________ ________ ________
________ ________ ________

4 Many abbreviations are used in government. What do these abbreviations stand for?

PM ________ MHR ________
MP ________ GG ________

5 Write commonly used abbreviations for these words.

federal ________ government ________ representatives ________

6 Look up each word in a dictionary. Write a definition and the language each one comes from.

monarchy ______________________________

____

democracy ______________________________

____

Tip A word that is spelt the same as another but has a different meaning is called a **homograph**. The noun *bear*, meaning *a big furry mammal*, is a homograph of the verb *bear*, meaning *to endure* or *to carry*.

7 These words are **homographs**. Think of two different meanings for each word. Write a sentence to show each meaning.

premier: 1. ______________________________

2. ______________________________

cabinet: 1. ______________________________

2. ______________________________

minister: 1. ______________________________

2. ______________________________

8 Add **affixes** to the base word to form related words.

depend ______________________________

democrat ______________________________

oppose ______________________________

federal ______________________________

elect ______________________________

9 Write the correct form of list words to complete the passage.

Most countries are ______________. In these countries, the citizens ______________ their government. In one type of democracy, such as in Australia and Singapore, the government is headed by a prime ______________. In another type of democracy, such as in the United States and France, the government is headed by a ______________. The role of the ______________ is to question government decisions and propose alternative policies.

Answer: c

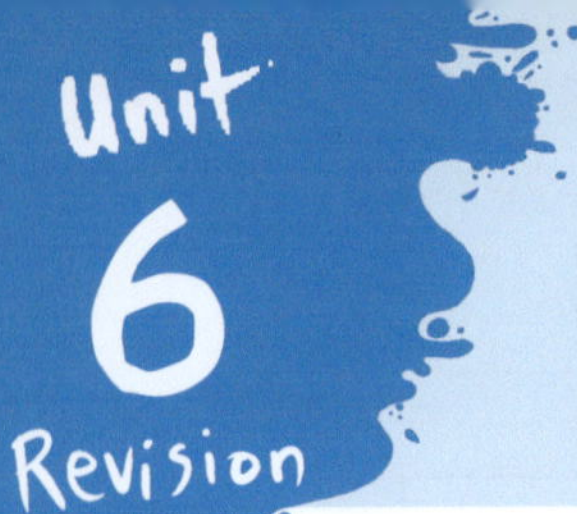

What is your problem if you are suffering from verbiage?

a you are constantly making up new verbs
b you are allergic to the smell of rotting vegetables
c you use many redundant words

1 Complete the table.

verb	add ed	add ing	noun
persuade	persuaded		
exhibit			exhibition
digest			digestion
admit		admitting	
decide	decided		
guarantee	guaranteed		
invert		inverting	

2 Write double letters to complete each word.

a __ __ociation   o __ __osition   pa __ __enger   permi __ __ion   cha __ __enge
c __ __peration   co __ __i __ __ __ __   __ __rie   a __ __reciation   admi __ __ion

3 Write g or j.

pre __udice   ad __acent   refu __ee   ur __ent   fra __ile   jud __e

4 Write the missing letter or letters that make the s or sh sound.

rejoi __e   appre __ia __ __on   adju __tment   exten __ __on
revolu __ __on   prejudi __e   exhibi __ __on   justi __e
democra __y   expan __ __on

5 Rearrange the letters to make an appropriate word.

I received a tintiondisc in the competition. ________________
As time ran out, the teams played with increasing spontraidee. ________________
Japan has the oldest chomanyr in the world. ________________
I'm good at basketball but only gaverea in swimming. ________________
Granddad has to go to the doctor to renew his pitcrosprine. ________________
When the weather is cool, we like to sit out on the rahdenva. ________________

6 Use the clues to complete the puzzle.

1.											E
2.											E
3.								E			
4.									E		
5.										E	
6.									E		
7.			E								
8.						E					
9.					E						

1. enemy
2. run away from
3. first public appearance
4. needed immediately
5. group of senior government ministers
6. next to
7. Darwin's theory of ___________
8. something that is owned
9. working well together

7 Add a suitable prefix.

____digestion ____advantage ____justice ____decision ____judge

8 Proofread this text. The text has six words that are incorrect. Circle the mistakes. Then write the correct spelling of the words in the boxes.

I knew the little cakes on the bench were for morning tea and I would never get permition to have one now. Maybe the solussion was to sneak a couple while no one was around, and avoid detecsion. I had one in my hand when Dad came into the kitchen, so I stuffed it in my mouth. Eating that quickly is bad for the digeston! I've made a resolusion not to do it again, because it's worse than making an admition with your mouth full!

9 Use the anagram to write a list word that matches the definition.

anagram	word	definition
car comedy	____________	government by the people
green	____________	text type
jab until	____________	extremely joyful
toenail trail	____________	device where words begin with the same sound
moo quits	____________	an insect with an itchy bite
bean tic	____________	furniture to display items
cool is nil	____________	crash
red leaf	____________	government where power is shared with the states
so drive in	____________	distraction

Answer: c

Unit 7

Which shape is **sym**metrical?

a 

b 

c 

Say Listen Look Understand Remember Practise

synthesise	____________
idio**syn**crasy	____________
syndrome	____________
sympathy	____________
symbiotic	____________
symmetry	____________
coherent	____________
cohesive	____________
coincidence	____________
coordinate	____________
ac**com**modate	____________
commotion	____________
compensate	____________
correlate	____________
collaborate	____________

Tip The unstressed vowel sound is called a **schwa**. This sound can be written in many ways.
away animal literal bitten action kingdom evil

1 For each list word, underline the letters that make the **schwa**. Not every word contains a schwa.

synthesise	idiosyncrasy	syndrome
sympathy	symbiotic	symmetry
coherent	cohesive	coincidence
coordinate	accommodate	commotion
compensate	correlate	collaborate

2 Write your name and underline the **schwa** if there is one.

____

Tip **com-** and **syn-** mean *with* or *together*. **com-** is Latin in origin and **syn-** is Greek in origin.

3 Use a dictionary to write the word origins. Then answer the question.

syndrome: syn (together) + ____________ = a set of symptoms that go together to indicate a disease

sympathy: sym (together) + ____________ = the sharing of another person's emotions

symbiotic: sym (together) + ____________ = dependent on each other; living together

symmetry: sym (together) + ____________ = where one side is the same as the other

When does **syn-** change to **sym-**?

____

Use **com-** before **b**, **p** or **m**. Use **col-** before **l**. Use **cor-** before **r**.
Use **co-** before **h** or **gn**. Use **con-** in all other cases.

4 Write **com**, **col**, **cor**, **co** or **con** to finish each word.

_____lect	re_____gnise	_____cave	_____pany
_____dolence	_____herent	_____pliment	_____ment
_____bine	_____respond	_____league	_____fident

5 Write two list words that mean *work together.* ____________________ ____________________

6 Use list words to complete the puzzle.

7 Write a list word that matches the definition.

____________________ behaviour unique to a person

____________________ housing; a place to live

____________________ disturbance; noise

____________________ events happening together

Answer: b

Unit 8

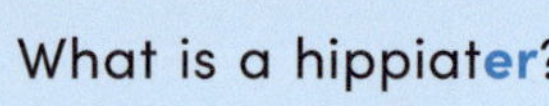

What is a hippiat**er**?

a a hip surgeon
b a species of alligator
c a horse doctor

Say Listen Look Understand Remember Practise

coach ______
pilot ______
lifeguard ______
locksmith ______
optician ______
treasurer ______
choreographer ______
courier ______
tutor ______
sculptor ______
surgeon ______
analyst ______
pharmacist ______
athlete ______
paramedic ______

1 Complete the table.

occupation	base word
engineer	
treasurer	
	law
	account
	pharmacy
scientist	
analyst	
translator	
	politic

2 Write the two list words that are also compound words.

______ ______

3 Write a list word that fits each group.

nurse anaesthetist ______ doctor

artist painter illustrator ______

optometrist ophthalmologist ______

teacher lecturer ______ professor

4 Write the occupation of a person who works in each place.

laboratory ______
restaurant ______
beach ______
aeroplane ______
ambulance ______
art studio ______

Spelling Rules! Student Book 6 (ISBN 9780655092636) © Janelle Ho, Helen Pearson

5 *Optos* is Greek for *seen, visible*; *opsis* means *a sight*. Write the meanings of the related words. Underline the part of the word that comes from *optos* or *opsis*.

optician ______________________________

optical ______________________________

synopsis ______________________________

autopsy ______________________________

6 Use a dictionary to write the meanings of the root words. What language is the root word in?

athlon ______________________________

medeor ______________________________

7 Write a word to match the definition. The root word is given.

an event consisting of ten challenges (*athlon*) ______________

the science of restoring or maintaining health (*medeor*) ______________

someone trained to help a doctor as part of a rescue team (*medeor*) ______________

8 Add **er**, **eer**, **or**, **ian** or **ist** to complete these occupation names. Use a dictionary if you need help.

design______	anaesthet______	music______
curat______	carpent______	zoolog______
mountain______	guitar______	librar______
edit______	electric______	invent______
ornitholog______	plumb______	engine______

9 The text has six words that are incorrect. Circle the mistakes. Then write the correct spelling of the words in the boxes.

I enjoy watching the Olympic Games. The venu is usually colourful, with the many flags of the participating nations. The atheletes exibit great skill and courage as they persue their dreams and the crowds cheer their appresiation. I feel I am always guranteed great entertainment.

10 *Coach* can be both a noun and a verb. Write a sentence for each meaning of the word.

coach (noun): ______________________________

____

coach (verb): ______________________________

____

Answer: c

Unit 9

Risibility is the ability to:

a rise early
b laugh easily
c rotate your wrists

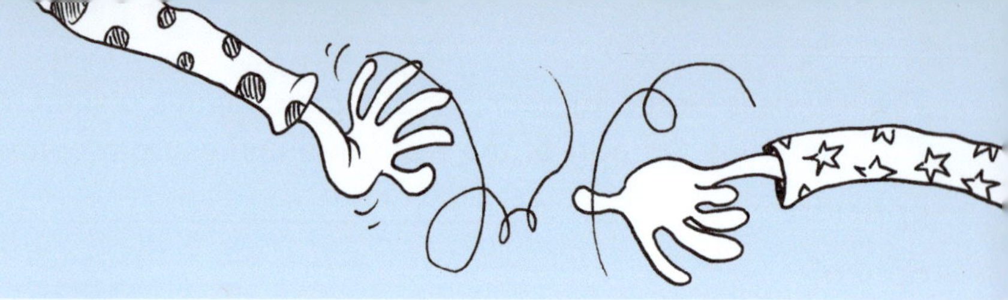

Say Listen Look Understand Remember Practise

durability	______
probability	______
acceptability	______
compatibility	______
predictability	______
variability	______
changeability	______
irritability	______
visibility	______
flexibility	______
vulnerability	______
accessibility	______
invincibility	______
eligibility	______
susceptibility	______

Tip

Words ending in **ible** and **able** are adjectives. These words may also add **ity** as a second suffix.
Adding **ity** changes the adjective to a noun.

1 Write the list words ending in **ibility**. Then write the adjectival form.

noun	adjective

2 Write the list words ending in **ability**. Then write the adjectival form.

noun	adjective

noun	adjective

3 Write the list word in which silent **e** has been kept when the suffixes are added to the base word.

______

Another word that keeps silent **e** is *traceability*. Why do these words keep the silent **e**?

______

Spelling Rules! Student Book 6 (ISBN 9780655092636) © Janelle Ho, Helen Pearson

4 Use each clue to find a smaller word within a list word. Write the small word and the list word.

clue	answer	list word
the opposite of *out*	______	______
what thieves do	______	______
the colour of anger or embarrassment	______	______
what you do to show off your muscles	______	______
tap gently with affection	______	______

5 Add **un**, **im**, **in** or **ir** to make an antonym.

____flexibility	____probability	____predictability	____responsibility
____reliability	____ability	____suitability	____compatibility
____eligibility	____regularity	____visibility	____likeability

6 Write a list word that ends in **ibility** or **ability**.

Cyber criminals look for a ______________ so they can hack into the system.

Lili avoids ______________ and constantly surprises us with new magic tricks.

Our bushwalk was cancelled due to the ______________ of a thunderstorm.

Buster, our dog, has been bad-tempered recently. Our vet discovered that his ______________ was due to an ear infection.

The ______________ criteria for the award are listed on the council website.

It is the ______________ of superheroes that we most want!

______________ to buildings is important for people with mobility problems.

7 Make a noun from each adjective. What does each noun mean?

	noun	meaning
stable	______	______
audible	______	______
durable	______	______
feasible	______	______
manoeuvrable	______	______

Answer: b

Unit 10

What is tricho**logy**?

a the science of hair and its diseases
b the knowledge of three-sided objects
c the study of tricks

Say **L**isten **L**ook **U**nderstand **R**emember **P**ractise

environment	______
rainforest	______
pollution	______
greenhouse	______
climate	______
recycle	______
ozone	______
ecology	______
irrigation	______
conservation	______
deforestation	______
flora	______
fauna	______
sustainable	______
atmosphere	______

1 Write the affixes used in the list words.

suffixes ______ ______
______ ______

prefixes ______
______

2 Write the base words.

pollution ______
irrigation ______
conservation ______
sustainable ______
recycle ______
emission ______

3 Write the list words that are compound words.

______ ______

Tip

Prefixes and suffixes (affixes) add to the meaning of a base word.
de + *forest* + *ation* = the process of getting rid of forests

4 Write the meanings of these words. Use a dictionary if you need help.

reforestation ______
unsustainable ______
pollutants ______

5 Use each clue to find a smaller word within a list word. Write the small word and the list word.

clue	answer	list word
a 3D shape	______	______
a number	______	______
a discoloured patch	______	______
where a train stops	______	______

Spelling Rules! Student Book 6 (ISBN 9780655092636) © Janelle Ho, Helen Pearson

6 Use some of the letters in each list word to make a three-letter, a four-letter and a five-letter word.

	environment	**irrigation**	**sustainable**
3 letters	____________	____________	____________
4 letters	____________	____________	____________
5 letters	____________	____________	____________

7 Use list words to complete the diagram. Briefly explain the diagram.

____________ + ____________ → the ____________ effect → ____________ change and rising sea levels

____

____

____

Tip

logy is a word element that means *science* or *the study of.*
bio (living things) + *logy* → *biology*

8 Use a dictionary to find the meaning of each word. Write the meaning, then use the word in a sentence.

ecology ____

____

psychology ____

____

zoology ____

____

meteorology ____

____

9 Use a list word to name each category. Add more examples.

____________: trees, shrubs, grass, ____________, ____________

____________: mammals, insects, fish, ____________, ____________

____________: hose, dam, water pipe, ____________, ____________

Answer: a

Unit 11

"*Terra* means *earth* or *land*."

What does *tetra* mean?

a test
b shape
c four

Say Listen Look Understand Remember Practise	
biology	________
biography	________
autobiography	________
biodegradable	________
microbe	________
zoology	________
zoophobia	________
anthropology	________
philanthropy	________
anthropomorphism	________
geology	________
geography	________
terrace	________
terrain	________
terrestrial	________

Tip

The suffixes **-logy** and **-graphy** show area of study. **-logy** means *science* or *the study of*. **-graphy** is used for art or a science that describes a subject.

1 Write **-logy** or **-graphy**.

photo________	bio________
techno________	choreo________
meteoro________	geo________
etymo________	cinemato________
oceano________	psycho________
eco________	ornitho________
genea________	palaeonto________

2 **bio-** and **geo-** can add both **-logy** and **-graphy**. Write the meanings of the words.

biology ________________________________

biography ________________________________

geology ________________________________

geography ________________________________

3 Write the meanings of each element in the word.

biodegradable = bio + de + grade + able

= ____________ + ____________ + ____________ + ____________

microbe = micro + bio

= ____________ + ____________

anthropomorphism = anthropo + morph + ism

= ____________ + ____________ + ____________

Anthropomorphism is a technique in which animals or gods are given human qualities.
My cat felt sorry when I hurt myself.

4 Use anthropomorphism to write a story about animals.

____

____

____

____

____

5 Write the occupation.

biology	zoology	geology	anthropology
________	________	________	________
biography	geography	philanthropy	
________	________	________	

6 *Terra* means *earth* or *land*. Rearrange the letters to write a word that has the root word *terra*.

We went out onto the ____________ (ractree) to look at the night sky.

Our ____________ (rireret) barks if there's a full moon.

In our solar system, Venus, Mars, Mercury and Earth are ____________ (lateristerr) planets.

Australia has six states and ten ____________ (rortisetire).

The ____________ (rainter) is rocky, so walkers should take extra time.

7 The word *phobia* means *extreme fear*. What phobias can you think of?

____

____

Answer: c

Unit 12 Revision

What is a snott**er**?

a a rope attached to a ship's mast
b a person with a cold
c a sick pig

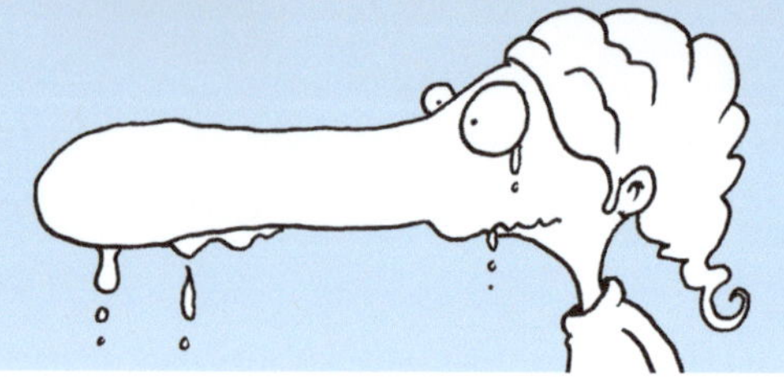

1 Write the letters that make the **schwa** sound.

clim__te desp__at__n cabin__t prej__dice biol__gy

sculpt__ couri__ opp__tun__ty coher__nt surg__n

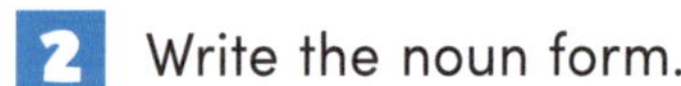

2 Write the noun form.

disturb __________ decide __________
expand __________ accept __________
transmit __________ translate __________
possess __________ govern __________

3 Write an occupation associated with each picture.

____

____

____

____

4 Use a prefix to make the antonym.

permanent __________ certainty __________ flexibility __________
relevant __________ possibility __________ stability __________

5 Use each word in a sentence.

invisibility ______________________________

invincibility ______________________________

6 Colour the correct word.

Fireworks have a terrible | affect | effect | on my dog, who howls and whimpers.

Dad's taking me to buy some | stationary | stationery | for my project.

I had to | practice | practise | for weeks before I could hold my | breath | breathe | long enough to swim across the pool underwater.

The charity shop | accepts | excepts | all donations | accept | except | furniture.

Spelling Rules! Student Book 6 (ISBN 9780655092636) © Janelle Ho, Helen Pearson

7 Rewrite each sentence using one word to replace the underlined word or phrase.

Pulling at his hair when he is nervous is his behaviour that identifies him.

____

Airports must close if fog reduces the ability to see.

____

We put our empty bottles in the yellow bin so that they can be made into something else.

____

The world has to be careful about getting rid of all the forests, or our way of life may not be able to be sustained.

____

____

Police were called to calm a noisy disturbance at the store.

____

The actor's story of her own life is eagerly anticipated.

____

8 Write the correct form of the verb to complete each sentence.

Our team captain later ______________ (accept) responsibility for mixing up the time of our match.

Yesterday, Alan ______________ (admit) that he used to believe in bunyips.

Everyone had to ______________ (cooperate) to complete the obstacle course.

Were you ______________ (disturb) by the thunderstorm last night?

______________ (change) my shirt at half time definitely helped me play better.

Joey ______________ (sympathy) with me when he heard my gerbil was ill.

9 Write about a job you might like to have as an adult.

____

____

____

Answer: a

Unit 13

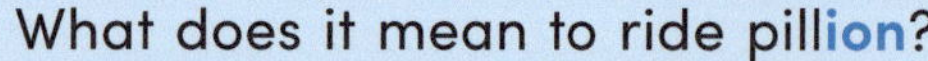

What does it mean to ride pillion?

a to be a passenger on a motorcycle
b to deliver medicines in a van
c to carry pillows on a bike

Say Listen Look Understand Remember Practise	
prior	______________
senior	______________
superior	______________
exterior	______________
posterior	______________
deteriorate	______________
median	______________
alliance	______________
valiant	______________
pliant	______________
ruffian	______________
peculiar	______________
plagiarise	______________
matriarch	______________
diarrhoea	______________

1 Write a list word that rhymes.

fire ______________
defiance ______________
giant ______________
idea ______________

2 Write the list word that is an antonym.

junior ______________
inferior ______________
disunity ______________
interior ______________
ordinary ______________

3 Write the list word that is a synonym.

union ______________
decline ______________
courageous ______________
forge ______________

Tip *Interior, exterior, posterior* and *anterior* describe different positions. The first syllable indicates the position.

4 Complete each sentence.

If *postpone* means *put off until later*, then **post** means ______________.
If *antenatal* means *before birth*, then **ante** means ______________.
If *external* means *outside*, then **ex** means ______________.
If *internal* means *inside*, then **in** means ______________.

The interior is warmer than the exterior.

5 Draw a line to match each word to its meaning.

interior	before
exterior	inside
anterior	behind
posterior	outside

Spelling Rules! Student Book 6 (ISBN 9780655092636) © Janelle Ho, Helen Pearson

A **mnemonic** helps you remember something tricky.
*Bring your **ears** to reh**ears**als.*
*There is **a rat** in sep**arat**e.*

6 Make up a mnemonic to help you remember the spelling of *diarrhoea*.

Many of the list words add **ity** to make the noun.
prior → priority

7 Add **ity** to make the noun.

prior ______	senior ______
inferior ______	peculiar ______
superior ______	familiar ______

8 **sen** is a root word meaning *old.* Circle the word in each pair that has that root word. Then write a sentence that uses that word.

senior sender ______
sensible senator ______
sensation senile ______
______

9 Use the clues to complete the puzzle. If there is no clue, the word is a list word. Write your own clue for that word.

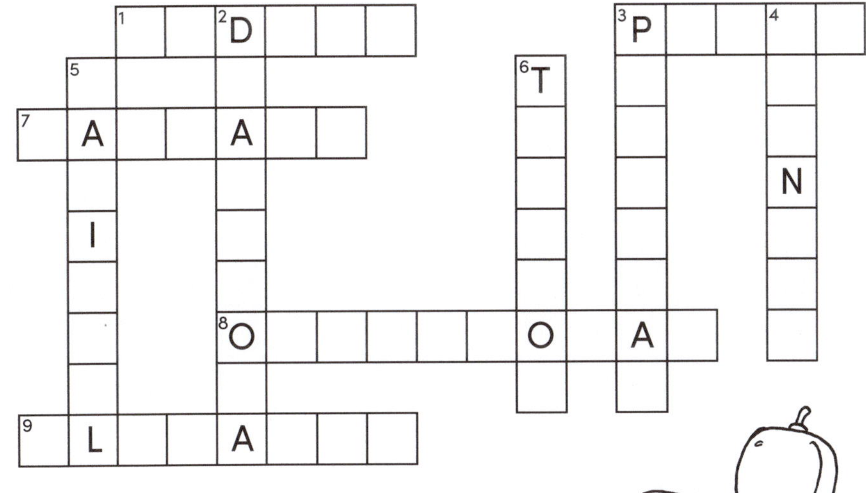

Across

1. ______
3. ______
7. giving out or reflecting light
8. once in a while
9. ______

Down

2. ______
3. ______
4. a point of view
5. logical
6. teaching or instruction

Answer: a

If a **sequel** follows the main story, what comes before the main story?

a a forequel
b a prequel
c a subquel

Say Listen Look Understand Remember Practise	
telescope	______
periscope	______
aspect	______
suspect	______
auspicious	______
conspicuous	______
despise	______
despicable	______
spectacle	______
speculate	______
sequence	______
sequel	______
execute	______
prosecute	______
consecutive	______

Etymology is the study of the origin of words.

spek is a root word that means *to observe*. It is found in the Latin word *scopium* and in the Greek word *skopein*, which mean *to look at* or *examine*.

1 Write the list words that have *skopein* in their etymology.

______

______

2 **-scope** is used to indicate a viewing instrument. Write the meanings of the other word parts.

telescope: an instrument that makes distant objects appear closer

tele: ______

periscope: an instrument for viewing objects that are not in direct sight

peri: ______

Spek is also found in the Latin word *specere*, which means *to look*.

3 Write the list words that have *specere* in their etymology. You may consult your dictionary.

______ ______ ______ ______

______ ______ ______ ______

Spelling Rules! Student Book 6 (ISBN 9780655092636) © Janelle Ho, Helen Pearson

4 Add an affix to make a word from the same word family. Make sure your word is from a different grammatical class.

despise ______________ auspicious ______________

spectacular ______________ suspect ______________

execute ______________ consecutive ______________

Tip *Sequi* is a Latin word that means *to follow.*

5 Write the list words that have *sequi* in their etymology.

______________ ______________ ______________

______________ ______________

6 *sequel*, *sequence* and *consecutive* are closely related in meaning. Use each word in a sentence. Can you write a short text using all three words?

____

____

____

7 A malapropism is an inaccurate use of similar sounding words. Circle the malapropism in each sentence and write the correct word.

Our teacher asked us to spectacle on what will happen next in the story. ______________

The police plan to execute the criminal on charges of identity theft. ______________

Grace is so tall that she is conscientious wherever she goes. ______________

The consecutive of the injury was that the team had to play without their captain. ______________

Smashing the windows of the care home is disposable! ______________

Tip Some nouns appear only in the plural form. *spectacles* *trousers* *scissors*

8 Write a plural-only noun to complete each sentence.

My cousins live on the ______________ of town on a large block.

When you are packing for the camp, check that all your ______________, including your ______________, are tagged with your name.

______________ on winning the poetry contest!

Would you mind using your ______________ or turning down the volume?

Use the ______________ to get the meat off the barbecue.

Answer: b

Unit 15

What does vertiginous mean?

a vertical
b whirling
c a virtual reality game show

Say Listen Look Understand Remember Practise	
wondrous	______
perilous	______
miraculous	______
Indigenous	______
cantankerous	______
ferocious	______
gregarious	______
rebellious	______
voracious	______
precarious	______
instantaneous	______
spontaneous	______
righteous	______
continuous	______
ambiguous	______

Tip Sometimes the base word changes when **ous** is added.

1 Look at the **-ous** word. Write the related base word, then state the change to the base word.

base word	-ous word	change to base word
	wondrous	delete ___
	humorous	delete ___
	miraculous	change le to ___
	studious	change ___ to ___
	rebellious	double ___

2 Write four list words in which you can see the whole base word.

______ ______
______ ______

Rule If the base word ends in **ce** or **y**, change **e** or **y** to **i** before adding **ous**.
fury → furious *vice → vicious*

3 Add **ous**.

study ______ grace ______ glory ______
envy ______ mystery ______ luxury ______
malice ______ space ______ fury ______

Rule If the base word ends in **e**, drop the **e** before adding **ous**. *fame → famous*
Exception: some words ending in **ge** *courage → courageous*

4 Add **ous**.

ridicule ______ continue ______ outrage ______
carnivore ______ courage ______ advantage ______

Spelling Rules! Student Book 6 (ISBN 9780655092636) © Janelle Ho, Helen Pearson

Similes describe something by comparing it to something else using *like* or *as*.
The old building looked as precarious as a house of cards.

5 Write a simile for each word: *suspicious, gregarious, miraculous.*

____

____

____

6 Write the list word that is a synonym. What does the final word mean?

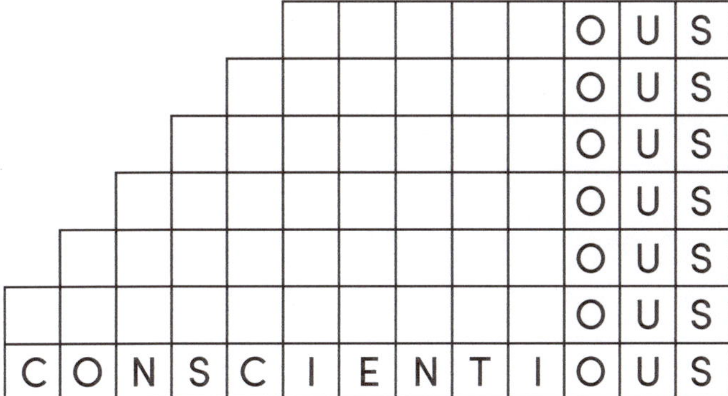

dangerous
greedy
Aboriginal
impulsive
grumpy
immediate

____

7 Use each clue to find a smaller word within a list word. Write the small word and the list word.

clue	answer	list word
something you can ring	______	______
a browning of the skin	______	______
first in a race	______	______
a passenger vehicle	______	______
pro and ...	______	______
large	______	______
move soil with a spade	______	______

8 The words **Indigenous** and **Aboriginal** are sometimes used as if they mean the same thing. Find out the difference and explain it in your own words.

____

____

____

Answer: b

Unit 16

What does the word element **neo** mean?

a nil
b new
c a broken neon light

Say Listen Look Understand Remember Practise

novel ______
novelty ______
novice ______
innovate ______
innovation ______
vocal ______
vocabulary ______
advocate ______
vociferous ______
invoke ______
provoke ______
notice ______
notify ______
annotate ______
reminisce ______

1 Sort the list words into adjectives, verbs and nouns. Some words may belong to more than one group.

verbs

______ ______
______ ______
______ ______
______ ______

nouns

______
______
______
______
______
______
______

adjectives

______
______
______

Tip Most English words have Old English, Latin or Greek origins. Synonyms often have different origins. For example, *new* is from Old English, while *novel* is from Latin. The Latin origins for the list words are:

nova = new *vox* = voice *notare* = note *reminisci* = remember

2 Group the list words.

related to **voice**:

______ ______
______ ______
______ ______

related to **remember**:

______

related to **new**:

______ ______
______ ______
______

related to **note**: ______

______ ______

3 Using the word origin as a clue, write a list word to match each definition.

speaking with a loud, fierce voice ____________

someone new and inexperienced ____________

to produce something new ____________

to call forth ____________

to make notes ____________

to remember the past ____________

to speak on someone's behalf ____________

something new and unusual ____________

4 These words belong to the same word family as list words. Use each word in a sentence to show its meaning. Choose another list word and write a related word and sentence of your own.

renovation: ________________________________

notorious: ________________________________

revoke: ________________________________

reminiscent: ________________________________

____________ ________________________________

Tip **Novel** is a homograph. It has two different meanings.

5 Write a definition for each meaning of *novel*.

novel (noun) = ________________________________

novel (adjective) = ________________________________

6 Use a list word to complete each title. Make up a title and author of your own.

A Complete ____________ by B Ginner

____________ No More! by I Forget

____________ in the Home by Han D Man

The ____________ Speaker by IM Noisy

Creating a Great ____________ by Rider Book

________________________ by ____________

Answer: b

Unit 17

What is an important rule when you're in a **laboratory**?

a Be careful!
b Have fun!
c Try everything!

Say Listen Look Understand Remember Practise

solution	______________
toxic	______________
method	______________
experiment	______________
acid	______________
alkaline	______________
temperature	______________
evaporate	______________
thermometer	______________
theory	______________
equipment	______________
chemical	______________
microscope	______________
hypothesis	______________
laboratory	______________

1 Divide these list words into syllables. Underline the syllable that is stressed in each word.

method	alkaline
evaporate	equipment
microscope	hypothesis
temperature	acid

Rule

ic is a less common suffix that changes a noun to an adjective. The base word usually changes when **ic** is added.

tragedy → tragic

2 Add **ic** to make the adjective. The base word may change. Use a dictionary if you need help.

noun	adjective
base	
acid	
toxin	
science	
horror	

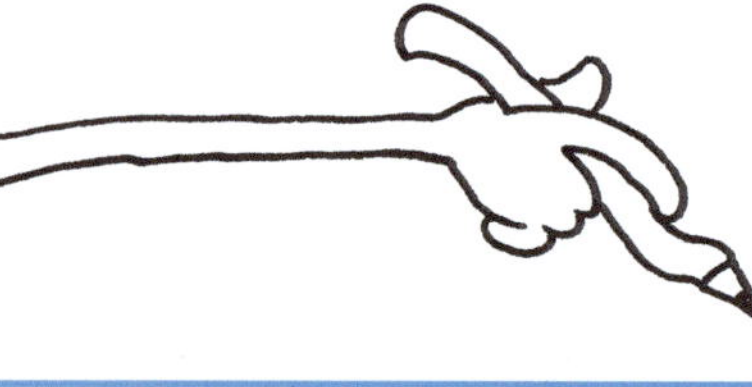

Tip

In a compound word, both parts can be used independently. Some words are not compound words, but consist of two separate word elements. **Scope** and **meter** can act as words and as word elements. As word elements, **scope** refers to a viewing instrument and **meter** to a measuring instrument.

3 Use a dictionary to find the meaning of the word element and the whole word.

micro = ______________ microscope = ______________

thermo = ______________ thermometer = ______________

Write other words you know that use these word elements.

scope: ______________

meter: ______________

Spelling Rules! Student Book 6 (ISBN 9780655092636) © Janelle Ho, Helen Pearson

4 Write the correct form of a list word to complete each sentence.

What usually makes people sick are ________________ creatures called viruses and bacteria.

When you bake a cake, it is very important to follow the ________________ given in the recipe.

Some ________________ are poisonous. Bottles containing dangerous materials are usually labelled ________________.

My teacher believes that any place can be a ________________. She encourages us to carry out ________________ to test things out. I am going to test my ________________ that the warmer the room, the quicker a slice of apple goes brown.

5 Use list words to complete the puzzle.

Across

6. a room in which experiments are performed
8. a way of explaining what is observed
9. a way of testing a theory

Down

1. a measure of how hot or cold something is
2. a solution is either neutral, acidic or ________
3. good experiments follow the scientific ________
4. to convert a liquid into a gas
5. what is tested during an experiment
7. vinegar is a common ________
10. poisonous

6 Write whether these word pairs are similar or different in meaning.

acidic/alkaline ________________

evaporation/condensation ________________

hypothesis/theory ________________

equipment/apparatus ________________

theoretical/practical ________________

problem/difficulty ________________

Answer: a

Unit 18 Revision

The word quadrumanous is used to describe:

a lions that have four manes
b animals that use four feet as hands
c animals that have four teeth for eating

1 Complete the tables.

noun	adjective
miracle	
advantage	
humour	
mystery	
peculiarity	
essence	
practice	

verb	noun
edit	
equip	
solve	

verb	adjective
despise	
rebel	
innovate	

2 Write words that follow each rule.

Remove silent **e** from the base word before adding a suffix.

____

Change the final **y** to **i** before adding a suffix.

____

Keep the **e** so the **g** sound stays soft when adding a suffix.

____

3 Write the correct form of the verb to complete each sentence.

Dad was ____________ (notify) that he has jury duty next month.

Uncle Carlos ____________ (rebel) against all the rules when he was young but now he's a police inspector!

I love the cakes at Pierre's Patisserie because they are always ____________ (experiment) with new flavours.

Did you know that if you drink too much water, you can get water ____________ (poison)?

Because the water ____________ (evaporate) as soon as it hit the pan, I knew the pan was hot.

At Christmas, our two sets of grandparents love ____________ (reminisce) about their childhoods.

Spelling Rules! Student Book 6 (ISBN 9780655092636) © Janelle Ho, Helen Pearson

4 Use a word you have learnt to complete each sentence.

Galileo Galilei was the first person to use the ________________ to look at objects in the sky.

Anton van Leeuwenhoek was the first person to observe bacteria under a ________________.

You must take precautions when handling ________________ chemicals.

The best way to increase your ________________ is to read a lot.

A stomach bug gave Ramon a bad case of ________________.

Cherie is always happy to give her ________________ on any issue.

Tip When two or more words start with the same sound, it is called **alliteration**.

5 Write a second word to make an alliterative phrase.

hideous ________________	________________ occasion
peculiar ________________	________________ vehicle
spontaneous ________________	________________ laboratory

6 Write a word to name each category.

	car, truck, tractor, van
	granola, oats, porridge, muesli
	chlorine, ammonia, sodium chloride, fluoride

7 Proofread this text. The text has six words that are incorrect. Circle the mistakes. Then write the correct spelling of the words in the boxes.

The scientist was carrying out an experiment in her laborratory. She had a hypothises to test. Her method was to combine an acid and an alkali in different proportions and measure the temperature at which the solution boiled with a digital thermommeter. She wandered if the results would confirm her theorey that newtral solutions had the highest boiling point.

Answer: b

Unit 19

Flocculation is what happens when:

a music makes you sway from side to side
b flocks of sheep gather
c things are formed in a woolly mass

Say Listen Look Understand Remember Practise

definition	______________
repetition	______________
condemnation	______________
alteration	______________
interpretation	______________
continuation	______________
declaration	______________
cancellation	______________
inflammation	______________
explanation	______________
exclamation	______________
variation	______________
identification	______________
notification	______________
clarification	______________

1 Complete the table.

verb	noun
satisfy	
define	
	cancellation
	declaration
	exclamation
alter	
	repetition
	continuation

To add **ion** to a base word ending in **y**, change the **y** to **i** and add **cation**.
multiply → *multiplication*
Some exceptions: *vary* → *variation*
satisfy → *satisfaction*

2 Complete the table.

base word	add ion	base word	add ion
apply		notify	
multiply		magnify	
identify		clarify	

3 Write a list word.

This list word has a silent letter in its base word. ______________

This list word doubles the final consonant in its base word. ______________

4 Write the noun form for each verb. Say each pair aloud.

inflame ______________ classify ______________ define ______________

What happens to the stress on the final syllable? ______________________________

____

Spelling Rules! Student Book 6 (ISBN 9780655092636) © Janelle Ho, Helen Pearson

5 *Convert* and *converse* both form a noun ending in **ion**. Write the nouns, then use each one in a sentence. Use a dictionary if you need help.

convert ____________________

____

converse ____________________

____

6 Use the clues to complete the puzzle.

												Clue
						☐	☐	☐	I	O	N	all talk and no ___________
					☐	☐	☐	☐	I	O	N	learning with a tutor
				☐	☐	☐	☐	☐	I	O	N	The judge's ___________ is final.
			☐	☐	☐	☐	☐	☐	I	O	N	antonym of acceptance
		☐	☐	☐	☐	☐	☐	☐	I	O	N	what someone makes when they accuse you of something
	☐	☐	☐	☐	☐	☐	☐	☐	I	O	N	What is your ___________ for being late?
☐	☐	☐	☐	☐	☐	☐	☐	☐	I	O	N	document that informs you of something

Tip

An **abbreviation** is either a short form of a word, or the first letter of each word in a phrase.
government → *govt*   *United States of America* → *USA*
An **acronym** is a special kind of abbreviation. In an acronym, the abbreviation is pronounced as a whole word.
AIDS   *PIN*

7 Write the abbreviated name of each organisation. Circle the abbreviations that are acronyms.

United Nations Educational, Scientific and Cultural Organization ____________________
International Union for Conservation of Nature ____________________
Royal Society for the Prevention of Cruelty to Animals ____________________
North Atlantic Treaty Organization ____________________
National Aeronautic and Space Administration ____________________
International Crime Police Organization ____________________

8 What is odd about these phrases that contain an abbreviation?

ATM machine   HIV virus   PIN number

____

____

____

Answer: c

Unit 20

An aviary is where:

a aircraft are designed
b honey is harvested
c birds are kept

Say Listen Look Understand Remember Practise

military ________
anniversary ________
solitary ________
documentary ________
contrary ________
crockery ________
confectionery ________
surgery ________
nursery ________
treachery ________
forgery ________
sensory ________
contradictory ________
category ________
exploratory ________

1 Complete the table.

list word	adjective, noun or both?
crockery	
secondary	
nursery	
solitary	
treachery	
forgery	
anniversary	
military	

Some words can be pronounced in two ways and in one way, a syllable is not pronounced.
For example, *dormitory* can be pronounced as *daw-muh-tuh-ry* or *daw-muh-try*.
A syllable that is not pronounced is **elided**.

2 These words can be pronounced in two ways. Circle the syllable that can be elided.

category secretary jewellery desperate

3 Write a word ending in **ary** or **ery** to complete each advertising slogan.

PUT YOURSELF IN THE PICTURE!
Visit the National Portrait
____
today.

Drop in for a word or two with us at your local
________.

YUM!
____
THE HOME OF SWEETS

LITTLUNS
____
We'll look after your precious children

There's no present like the time!
Watch out for specials at Clocks 'n' Gems ________.

Spelling Rules! Student Book 6 (ISBN 9780655092636) © Janelle Ho, Helen Pearson

4 Write a list word that names the category.

__________ army, navy, air force

__________ cakes, sweets, chocolates

__________ plates, bowls, cups, saucers

__________ flowers, shrubs, saplings

Write a list word that is part of the category.

birthday, graduation, wedding, __________

fake, fraud, counterfeit, __________

classification, group, class, __________

pre-school, daycare centre, school, __________

Which word is used twice? __________

This word has two different meanings. Such a word is known as a __________.

5 Use *stationary* or *stationery* to complete each sentence.

The doors will not open until the bus is __________.

Where's the cheapest place to buy the __________ I need for school?

Some satellites are geo__________ in their orbit.

6 Add **ary**, **ery** or **ory**.

diction___	bound___	lavat___	secret___	laborat___	the___
hist___	imag___	lott___	burgl___	necess___	volunt___

7 Proofread this text. The text has five words that are incorrect. Circle the mistakes. Then write the correct spelling of the words in the boxes.

I love books, and one day I'd like to work in a libary. I think I'd enjoy putting each new book into its correct categry. I'm not sure what the salery would be. To become a librarian you have to finish secondory school first, and then go to university. I think I'll try doing work experience to make sure that the benefits aren't just imaginery!

Answer: c

Unit 21

An **ex**terminator is a:

a person who gets rid of pests
b character in a science fiction movie
c judge who decides who leaves a competition.

Say **L**isten **L**ook **U**nderstand **R**emember **P**ractise

enclose	______
engorge	______
entangle	______
extricate	______
exhale	______
excavate	______
exorbitant	______
precede	______
prelude	______
precursor	______
procession	______
prologue	______
procrastinate	______
proportion	______
postscript	______

1 Draw a line between each syllable and underline the stressed syllable.

enclose	engorge	entangle
extricate	exhale	excavate
exorbitant	precede	prelude
precursor	procession	prologue
procrastinate	proportion	postscript

2 Write the list words that have a schwa.

______ ______
______ ______
______ ______

3 Match the prefixes with their meanings. Then write a word that uses the prefix. Try not to use a list word.

prefix	**meaning**	**word**
en-	before	______
ex-	behind; after	______
pre-	in; into	______
pro-	out; out of	______
post-	for; forward; before	______

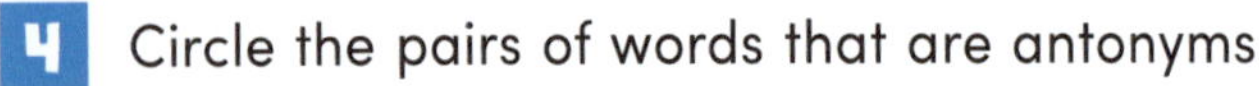

4 Circle the pairs of words that are antonyms.

entangle – disentangle	extricate – intricate	exhale – inhale
prelude – interlude	prologue – epilogue	precede – proceed
enclose – disclose	proportionate – disproportionate	

Spelling Rules! Student Book 6 (ISBN 9780655092636) © Janelle Ho, Helen Pearson

5 Write the list words that can add the given suffixes.

-ed, -ing

plural -s

-or

-al

-ion

-ment

6 Choose the correct word. Write a sentence that uses the word you do not choose.

The farmer | enclosed | enveloped | the land with a fence to keep the foxes out.

The author said that the first prize she won in Year 6 was the | prelude | prologue | to her writing career.

'Please | precede | proceed | to the hall to take your seats five minutes before the concert begins.'

The digger has started | excavating | extricating | the site, readying it for construction.

If you keep | postponing | procrastinating |, you will miss the deadline.

7 The word **entrance** is a homograph. It can be a noun or a verb. Write a sentence to show each meaning.

entrance (noun):

entrance (verb):

Answer: a

Unit 22

A heckel**phone** is:

a a loud heckler
b a noisy telephone
c a musical instrument

Say Listen Look Understand Remember Practise	
symphony	______
phonetic	______
microphone	______
cacophony	______
synonym	______
antonym	______
pseudonym	______
anonymous	______
empathy	______
telepathy	______
majesty	______
majority	______
magnify	______
magnificent	______
magnanimous	______

1 Write a list word that rhymes.

athletic ______
priority ______
synonymous ______

2 Write a list word that contains the smaller word.

net ______	cop ______
crop ______	ice ______
jest ______	one ______
pat ______ ______	cent ______
	or ______

3 Write whether these word pairs are synonyms or antonyms. Then write your own examples of synonyms and antonyms.

	synonyms or antonyms?	**your examples**
majority/most	______	______
magnanimous/petty	______	______

4 Write a word that has the same underlined word element.

<u>micro</u>phone ______ <u>maj</u>esty ______ <u>tele</u>pathy ______

5 Circle the meaning of each word element.

micro	loud	small	measure
magni	great	royal	magic
tele	sound	sender	far away

6 The meaning of each word element is given. **L** or **G** shows whether the word is from Latin or Greek. Write the list word that combines these word elements.

tele G: *far away*	+	patheia G: *feeling*	=	____________
kako G: *bad*	+	phone G: *sound*	=	____________
syn G: *together*	+	onyma G: *name*	=	____________
anti G: *opposite*	+	onyma G: *name*	=	____________
pseudo G: *false*	+	onyma G: *name*	=	____________
em L: *in*	+	patheia G: *feeling*	=	____________
poly G: *many*	+	phonic G: *sound*	=	____________
magnus L: *great*	+	animus L: *soul*	=	____________

7 Circle the malapropism in each sentence and write the correct word.

The magician claimed he used mental telegraphy to communicate with his assistant. ____________

The kidnapper sent a synonymous letter demanding a huge ransom. ____________

The authority of the class voted to play volleyball in the gym. ____________

Sam wears glasses to modify the text on his laptop. ____________

8 Rewrite each sentence using the correct form of a list word to make it shorter.

Dictionaries often use an alphabet in which symbols replace letters to represent pronunciation.

____

Being able to walk in others' shoes helps us understand them better.

____

Being on stage is scary because the silence makes every mistake seem bigger.

____

Answer: c

Unit 23

WHO is the abbreviation for:

a World Health Organization
b World Horticultural Organisation
c Wild Horses in the Outback

Say Listen Look Understand Remember Practise

medicine ______________
bacteria ______________
virus ______________
pregnant ______________
fracture ______________
organ ______________
influenza ______________
abdomen ______________
intestine ______________
capsule ______________
appendix ______________
vaccination ______________
immunisation ______________
pneumonia ______________
stethoscope ______________

1 Write list words to complete the table.

category	examples
	antibiotics, aspirin, ______________
medical equipment	syringe, thermometer, ______________
	heart, lungs, ______________
illnesses	bronchitis, tonsillitis, ______________

2 Write list words to answer the questions.

Which word has a silent letter? ______________

Which words end in the same vowel sound?

______________ ______________ ______________

Which words have a soft **c** sound?

______________ ______________

Which words contain double letters?

______________ ______________ ______________

3 Use each clue to find a smaller word within a list word. Write the small word and the list word.

clue	answer	list word
an assessment task	______________	______________
a shape like a hemisphere	______________	______________
a type of hat	______________	______________
a strong but tiny insect	______________	______________
a tool for writing	______________	______________
to play a part	______________	______________
rested on a chair	______________	______________

Spelling Rules! Student Book 6 (ISBN 9780655092636) © Janelle Ho, Helen Pearson

The word *organ* is a homograph. The word *appendix* is also a homograph. Each word has two very different meanings.

4 Write sentences to show the different meanings of *organ* and *appendix*. Use a dictionary if you need help.

organ 1. ______________________________

2. ______________________________

appendix 1. ______________________________

2. ______________________________

5 Say each word aloud. Which word does not belong? Why not?

chronic fracture medical stomach muscle ache bacteria

____

6 Write what each abbreviation stands for. Circle the abbreviations that are acronyms.

flu	______________	CF	______________
AIDS	______________	ADHD	______________
MS	______________	SIDS	______________

7 Each sentence contains one or two spelling errors. Circle the mistakes and write each word correctly.

I have a pain in my apendix so I have a docter's appointment. ______________ ______________

Salim fractured his wrist attempting to catch a cricket ball. ______________

We thought our cat's swelling addomen meant she was overweight, but it turned out she was pregnent. ______________ ______________

Nowadays children can be imunnised against many diseases. ______________

Why is it that even in hot whether a stethescope feels cold on your chest? ______________ ______________

If you have asthma, the wheeze makes it hard to breath. ______________

8 Write about a day in the life of a doctor. Use as many list words as you can.

____

____

____

____

Answer: a

Unit 24 Revision

What is sterilis**ation**?

a staring all the time
b the realisation that you do not like stairs
c the process of making something free of germs

1 Write the plural.

symphony ____________
multiple ____________
bacterium ____________
virus ____________
prologue ____________

2 Write the past tense.

vaccinate ____________
magnify ____________
cancel ____________
proceed ____________
yearn ____________

3 Add a suffix to each verb to complete the tables.

verb	noun
exclaim	
continue	
define	
satisfy	
repeat	

verb	noun
condemn	
vary	
document	
categorise	
enclose	

4 Write the list words from Units 19–23 that have silent letters.

____________ ____________ ____________

5 Name these instruments used by a doctor.

____

____

6 Write the double letters to complete each word.

va_ _ination a_ _iversary i_ _ovate a_ _endix
i_ _unisation a_ _elerate misce_ _aneous cance_ _ation

7 Fill in the letters that make the **schwa** sound.

tut___ treas___r___ nov___l c___coph___ny peril___s
s___pply pregn___nt exorbit___nt profess___n___l rep___tit___n

8 Add **ary**, **ery** or **ory**.

libr___ groc___ document___ forg___ summ___ explorat___
dormit___ jewell___ second___ gall___ imagin___ laborat___

Spelling Rules! Student Book 6 (ISBN 9780655092636) © Janelle Ho, Helen Pearson

9 Some letters have gone missing from each sentence. Write each sentence correctly.

At the begning of my project I have t includ a sumry.

____

Kara's favrit game is Monopoly becase she can be an imaginry millonaire.

____

Mr Jaffar is forgtful and somtimes throws his medcines away.

____

I was feeling mananimus so I forgave Rita for eating the majorty of the cofectionry.

____

10 Use the clues to complete the puzzle.

1.				A								
2.		A		A								
3.					A							
4.				A		A						
5.		A										
6.	A					A						
7.									A			
8.											A	

1. a musical instrument or body part
2. money for doing work
3. a place to borrow books
4. dig earth out
5. a series of loud grating noises
6. a charge made against you
7. a movie that gives information
8. speaking many languages

11 Write a word to complete each riddle.

Q: Why did the boy tiptoe past the medicine cabinet?
A: He didn't want to wake the ____________ tablets.

Q: Why is an optometrist like a teacher?
A: They both examine the ____________.

12 Write the correct form of each word to complete the sentences.

I fell down the stairs the other day and ____________ my ankle.
fracture

Roald is great at addition, subtraction and division, but not as good at ____________.
multiply

The rich ____________ ____________ helps readers to easily imagine the setting.
sense image

Answer: c

Unit 25

A **cygnet** is:

a a baby swan
b a tubular fishing net
c an internet expert

Say Listen Look Understand Remember Practise	
cyclone	______
cynical	______
cyberspace	______
urgency	______
accuracy	______
literacy	______
numeracy	______
privacy	______
pregnancy	______
diplomacy	______
adequacy	______
delicacy	______
obstinacy	______
buoyancy	______
legacy	______

1 Circle the word in which **cy** has a different sound.

cyclone   cynical   cyberspace

2 Use letters from each word to make a smaller word in which **c** has a hard sound. Use as many letters as you can.

cyclone	numeracy	obstinacy
______	______	______
pregnancy	**legacy**	**privacy**
______	______	______

3 Fill in words ending in **cy**.

The Chinese ______ is the yuan.
The motel's sign read 'No ______'.
The flood caused ______ evacuations.
A human ______ lasts about nine months.

Rule

Most nouns ending in **cy** have base words ending in **nt** or **te**.

infant → infancy   *delicate → delicacy*

4 Write the base word.

accuracy	urgency	obstinacy	buoyancy
______	______	______	______
privacy	**adequacy**	**numeracy**	**literacy**
______	______	______	______

5 What is the base word of **cy**nical? Use a dictionary to find a related word to complete each sentence.

A person who is cynical is called a ______.
A person who is cynical suffers from ______.

Spelling Rules! Student Book 6 (ISBN 9780655092636) © Janelle Ho, Helen Pearson

Cyber is a word element that shows that the word is related to computers.

6 Write a word beginning with **cyber** to match each definition.

_______________ a place where you can eat and use the internet at the same time

_______________ the irrational fear of computers or technology

7 Write list words.

Caviar is considered a _______________ in many countries.

Reading and writing are _______________ skills.

Air increases the _______________ of an inflatable object and helps it float.

People who value their _______________ often grow tall hedges.

_______________ Tracy caused great devastation in Darwin in 1974.

After practising archery for many months, my _______________ improved.

International _______________ resulted in a peace treaty.

The engineer advised that a new bridge should be built with _______________.

The prefix **ob** is Greek in origin and can mean either *towards* or *against*.

8 Each word in the puzzle begins with **ob**. Use a dictionary if you need help.

1.	O	B									
2.	O	B									
3.	O	B									
4.	O	B									
5.	O	B									
6.	O	B									
7.	O	B									
8.	O	B									
9.	O	B									
10.	O	B									

1. significantly overweight
2. to focus irrational attention on
3. to get or acquire
4. to watch closely
5. unclear or hidden
6. to put an obstacle in the way
7. out of date
8. clearly, evidently
9. an offensive or indecent word or remark
10. antonym of subjectivity

Answer: a

Unit 26

Psittacism is:

a an intelligent joke
b the habit of sitting around all the time
c meaningless, repetitive babble

Say Listen Look Understand Remember Practise

territory ____________
graffiti ____________
suppress ____________
pallor ____________
assassin ____________
apparatus ____________
millennium ____________
succulent ____________
eccentric ____________
gimmick ____________
dilemma ____________
pinnacle ____________
abbreviation ____________
etiquette ____________
intermittent ____________

1 Write each word as prefix + base word. What do you notice about the double letters?

unnecessary ____________
immigration ____________
irregular ____________
dissatisfied ____________
cooperation ____________
surreal ____________

2 Complete the table.

verb	add ing
suffocate	
suppress	
interrogate	
suffice	
recommend	
terrorise	

3 Underline the stressed syllable in each word.

territory intermittent graffiti pallor eccentric
etiquette curriculum succulent suppress apparatus

4 Sort the list words according to the number of syllables.

2
____
____
____

3
____
____
____
____
____
____
____

4
____
____
____
____

Which word is left?

____

Spelling Rules! Student Book 6 (ISBN 9780655092636) © Janelle Ho, Helen Pearson

5 Write a list word that is a synonym.

manners ______________

stunt ______________

peak ______________

6 Write one word for each period of time.

10 years ______________

100 years ______________

1000 years ______________

Tip

Nouns ending in **us** or **um** are Latin in origin. The Latin plural forms are still sometimes used. *radius → radii* *datum → data*

But nowadays most words add **s** or **es** to make the plural.

virus → viruses *vacuum → vacuums*

7 Write the plural without adding **s**. Use a dictionary to check your answer.

fungus	cactus	curriculum	millennium	crisis
______________	______________	______________	______________	______________

8 Which list word is French? ______________

9 Use the correct form of a list word to complete each sentence.

Many animals are ______________ by nature. Once they have established their ______________, they will fight others to protect it.

Both the peach and the nectarine look so ______________ that I have a ______________ about which to eat.

Meg found it hard to sleep because the streetlight outside her window would flash ______________.

Our school painted a mural on the fence to prevent ______________.

US President John F Kennedy was ______________ in Dallas in 1963.

The scientific ______________ in the laboratory included beakers, test tubes and Bunsen burners.

Tip

Collective nouns can be conventional or creative.

a school of fish *a wail of weeping willows*

10 Write creative collective nouns for *confetti* and *graffiti*. Then choose two words of your own and write collective nouns for them.

word	collective noun
confetti	
graffiti	

Answer: c

Unit 27

A **suf**fragette is a

a female supporter of women's voting rights
b person who suffers greatly
c female farmer who grows courgettes

Say Listen Look Understand Remember Practise	
subconscious	________
sublime	________
submerge	________
subordinate	________
subside	________
substandard	________
subterranean	________
subtle	________
succinct	________
succumb	________
suffocate	________
suppose	________
supplement	________
surreptitious	________
suspend	________

1 Write a list word that answers the questions.

Which two words have a silent letter?

________ ________

In which word is **cc** pronounced as in accelerate?

____

In which word is **cc** pronounced as in account?

____

Which two words have the same last syllable?

________ ________

Tip The prefix **sub-** means *under* or *less than*. The letter **b** may change to match the beginning consonant of the base word.

2 Write the correct spelling of the prefix **sub-**.

____total	____merge	____press
____cumb	____plement	____conscious
____pose	____port	____divide
____fix	____ficient	____scribe
____stance	____ceed	____ply

3 Colour A if the word is an adjective, V if the word is a verb or N if the word is a noun.

subconscious A V N	sublime A V N	submerge A V N
subordinate A V N	subside A V N	substandard A V N
subterranean A V N	subtle A V N	succinct A V N
succumb A V N	suffocate A V N	suppose A V N
supplement A V N	surreptitious A V N	suspend A V N

Spelling Rules! Student Book 6 (ISBN 9780655092636) © Janelle Ho, Helen Pearson

4 Write list words to complete the puzzle. Write your own clue for each word.

Down

1. ______________________
2. ______________________
4. ______________________
5. ______________________
7. ______________________
8. ______________________
9. ______________________
11. ______________________
12. ______________________

Across

2. ______________________
3. ______________________
6. ______________________
10. ______________________
13. ______________________
14. ______________________

5 Write list words to match the clues.

This word has a pet in it. ______________________

This word is below the earth. ______________________

This word goes underwater. ______________________

This word has a writing instrument in it. ______________________

This word is short and sweet. ______________________

This word is glorious. ______________________

This word is just not good enough. ______________________

Answer: a

Unit 28

A **dis**incentive is:

a a process that removes smells
b a machine that takes away your coins
c something that discourages you from doing something

Say Listen Look Understand Remember Practise	
incomprehension	
unmanageable	
discontinued	
ignorance	
invisibility	
irrational	
immobile	
immovable	
noticeably	
symmetrical	
unintentionally	
uncritically	
reversible	
illegibly	
predestined	

1 Add a prefix to make the antonym.

legible	mobile	visible
interested	necessary	rational
continue	critical	reversible

2 Add a suffix to make a noun.

ignore	press
exclude	visible
private	selfish
manage	criticise

3 Complete the table. The first word in each row is the base word. Add affixes to increase the number of syllables. The first one has been done for you.

Tip The general term for prefixes and suffixes is **affixes**.

1 syllable	2 syllables	3 syllables	4 syllables	5 syllables
		educate	educated	educational
	reverse			
	explore			
	intend			
note				
change				
please				

Spelling Rules! Student Book 6 (ISBN 9780655092636) © Janelle Ho, Helen Pearson

4 These sentences are too negative. Rewrite each sentence so it makes sense.

The note was not too illegible so Mum didn't know what I wanted.

____

Everyone looked puzzled as the conclusion to Rex's speech was not quite illogical.

____

The decision is irreversible if the manager disagrees with it.

____

The space in the hall was hard to rearrange as the chairs were not immovable.

____

The sale of the toy wasn't discontinued after complaints that it was not unsafe.

____

5 Write the correct form of the word to complete each sentence.

Reading ______________ (comprehend) is an important aspect of literacy.

In chapter 1, the author clearly indicates that the baby is ______________ (destiny) to be the hero.

A new family has moved in next door. There are two children and an ______________ (affection) puppy.

To encourage us in our fundraising this year, our teacher showed us a ______________ (document) about the cause we are supporting.

I ______________ (unintentional) trod on our cat's tail this morning.

Radio telescopes are an important part of the ______________ (explore) of space nowadays.

6 Proofread this text. The text has six words that are incorrect. Circle the mistakes. Then write the correct spelling of the words in the boxes.

I'm writing a detective story. My character, Shirl Lock, is a mischevious girl who loves solving mysteries. In the begining, her collection of semi-preceous gems goes missing. Her investergation leads her to view her best friend with suspision. In the end, however, her brother is the culprit. To apologise for his misbehaviour, he gives Shirl a beautiful piece of amber to add to her collection. In this story's sequal, the amber itself disappears.

Answer: c

Unit 29

What is a questionnaire?

a a person who asks pesky questions
b someone who doesn't know how much money they have
c a list of questions

Say Listen Look Understand Remember Practise

currency	______
exchange	______
pound	______
euro	______
rupiah	______
baht	______
allowance	______
financial	______
budget	______
discount	______
subsidy	______
purchase	______
expenditure	______
millionaire	______
treasury	______

1 Write each word as a base word and suffix.

millionaire = ______ + ______
allowance = ______ + ______
financial = ______ + ______
treasury = ______ + ______
accountant = ______ + ______

2 Write the plural.

allowance ______
currency ______
exchange ______
subsidy ______
euro ______

3 Some currencies have a special symbol. Write the currency.

¥ ______ ฿ ______
€ ______ £ ______

4 Write a rhyming word.

pound	euro	baht	millionaire
______	______	______	______

5 Use each clue to find a smaller word within a list word. Write the small word and the list word.

clue	small word	list word
helps fish steer	______	______
a flower not yet in bloom	______	______
to run after someone	______	______
king of the jungle	______	______
opposite of high	______	______
finish	______	______
a flat circular object	______	______

Spelling Rules! Student Book 6 (ISBN 9780655092636) © Janelle Ho, Helen Pearson

6 Write the correct form of the word to complete the sentence.

Toby was ______________ independent when he was eighteen.
(financial)

The T-shirt her aunt ______________ was too big, so she took it back to the shop to be ______________.
(purchase) (exchange)

Mrs Vazquez says ______________ is important so we know how much money we can spend without getting into debt.
(budget)

The boxes of chocolates were ______________ so Mr Muthu bought ten!
(discount)

Some generous parents are ______________ our excursion to Uluru.
(subsidy)

7 These people work with money. Write the occupation to match the definition.

accountant   cashier   teller   money changer

You pay this person at the checkout counter. ______________

You give or receive money from this person in a bank. ______________

This person exchanges one currency for another. ______________

This person keeps track of money in a business. ______________

8 Look at Alex's weekly account and write a report of his budget and expenditure.

Allowance	$20
Savings	$45.60
Magazine	$4.50
Grandma's gift	$7.50
Computer game	$6.95
Pool entry	$3.00
Ice cream	$2.70
	$24.65

____

____

____

____

____

____

Answer: c

To rappel is to:

a rap without a sense of rhythm
b descend a steep slope using a rope
c turn magnets away from each other

1 These words need single or double consonants added. Write the words correctly using the consonants in brackets.

su__u__ent (c, l) va__i__ation (c, n) a__o__odation (c, m)

a__a__in (s, s) gra__i__i (f, t) de__e__io__ate (t, r, r)

cu__i__u__um (r, c, l) a__e__ible (c, s) o__a__iona__y (c, s, l)

2 Write the plural.

territory committee millennium dilemma currency

__________ __________ __________ __________ __________

3 Most of the vowels have been left out of these sentences. Write each sentence correctly.

My sstr s xtrmly obstnt so w cn rrly prsd hr t chng hr mnd.

____

____

Prsnlly, I thnk m ncl is a lttl ccntrc bcs h njys rdng th dctnry.

____

____

I m rsrchng th dffrnc n tmpratur f bjcts dpndng on hw lng thy hve bn sbmrgd.

____

____

4 Write the correct form of the words to complete each sentence. You will need to add either one or two affixes.

Diana tried __________ (successful) to thread a needle and felt __________ (frustrate) when she pricked her finger yet ag

Faizal is an __________ (accomplish) __________ (violin). So far, his greatest __________ (achieve) has been __________ (perform) at the Town Hall.

As a result of food __________ (poison), her __________ (immune) was low and she __________ (succumb) to a bout of influenza.

Jill __________ (try) to claim __________ (ignore) but the judge was __________ (sympathy) and said her actions were __________ (excuse).

Spelling Rules! Student Book 6 (ISBN 9780655092636) © Janelle Ho, Helen Pearson

5 Write a word to match each definition. Each word has the letters **cy**, but not as a suffix.

hurricane ________________

use again ________________

two-wheeled transportation ________________

book of knowledge ________________

a conical, evergreen tree ________________

a poison ________________

6 Write a synonym and an antonym.

	synonym	antonym
buy	________________	________________
new	________________	________________
rational	________________	________________
sufficient	________________	________________

7 Write the correct form of the word to complete each sentence.

I closed my door to get some ________________.
private

Please check your work for ________________.
accurate

Snails are considered a ________________ in France.
delicate

Objects have greater ________________ in salt water than in fresh water.
buoyant

8 Add **c**, **cc**, **x** or **xc**.

o__upation	su__essful	e__ercise	de__ide
e__entric	re__eive	e__tra	a__entuate
e__ite	a__omplish	e__ept	e__act

9 Write as many words as you can by adding affixes to the base word. Choose one member of the word family to use in your own sentence.

able ____

____

believe ____

____

excite ____

____

Answer: b

Unit 31

A fascicle is:

a an interesting fact
b a broken icicle
c a small bundle

Say Listen Look Understand Remember Practise

ascend ______
descend ______
transcend ______
scenario ______
obscene ______
adolescent ______
fluorescent ______
iridescent ______
effervescent ______
miscellaneous ______
convalesce ______
scintillate ______
conscience ______
conscientious ______
resuscitate ______

1 Each word has a soft **c** sound. Use some of the letters in each word to make a word with a hard **c** sound.

obscene	miscellaneous
______	______
scenario	resuscitate
______	______

2 Write the list word that contains the smaller word.

dole	ran
______	______
ride	lane
______	______
it	science
______	______
scene	ale
______	______

Tip *Ascend*, *descend* and *transcend* all have the same Latin origin, *scandere*, meaning *to climb*. The prefix **a** or **ad** means *towards*, **de** means *away from* and **trans** means *beyond*.

3 Write what each word means. Use a dictionary to check your answer.

descend = ______
ascend = ______
transcend = ______

4 Use a word containing **sce** or **sci** and alliteration to invent a product name.

Erin's effervescent energy drink

______
______

Spelling Rules! Student Book 6 (ISBN 9780655092636) © Janelle Ho, Helen Pearson

5 These sets of words are sometimes confused. Write the correct word to complete each sentence.

ascent   accent   assent

The principal gave his ____________ to our plan to hold a twilight barbecue.

Don told the joke with a French ____________ to make us laugh.

The ____________ of Mount Everest must be made in stages.

descent   decent   dissent

She's got a ____________ singing voice but she's no opera singer!

Be careful, as the ____________ is steep and muddy.

There was no ____________ when Magda and Ewan were elected school captains.

6 Add the suffix to make the noun.

base word	add ion
fascinate	
resuscitate	

base word	add ity
susceptible	
obscene	

base word	add ence
convalesce	
effervesce	
transcend	
fluoresce	

7 Write the correct form of a list word to complete each sentence.

Grandma is ______________ well after her operation, although she is still ______________ to infection.

The dance troupe put on a ______________ performance at the concert. They wore ______________ costumes that appeared to glow in the spotlights.

The worst case ______________ has happened! Not only did Dad not contribute any ______________ items to our school's garage sale, but he bought even more junk home!

8 Write the list words that have meanings related to light. Use a dictionary if you need help.

____

Choose one of these words and use it in a sentence.

____

Answer: c

Unit 32

Syzygy is:

a a country near Kazakhstan
b the conjunction or opposition of two heavenly bodies
c the noise sausages make when you throw them on a barbecue

Say **L**isten **L**ook **U**nderstand **R**emember **P**ractise

onomatopoeia	______
asphalt	______
amateur	______
havoc	______
jargon	______
anemone	______
flummox	______
sleuth	______
nuisance	______
naive	______
pizzazz	______
eclipse	______
impromptu	______
labyrinth	______
conundrum	______

1 Sort the list words according to the number of syllables. Underline the stressed syllable in each word.

1 ______

2 ______
______
______
______
______
______
______
______

3 ______
______
______
______

4 ______

5 ______

2 Break the word into its base word and suffix.

skiing = ______ + ______
queued = ______ + ______
naively = ______ + ______

3 Write list words.

The new puppy caused ______ when it got into the grocery bags.

They discovered the pungent smell was caused by new ______ being put down on the road.

An ______ of the sun is an amazing natural event.

The poet uses ______ to express the storm's ferocity.

AMAZING

Tip

Mnemonics are tricks to help you remember something more easily.
*Eclipse – it **clips** from **e** to **e**.* *With asthma, each breath is hard.*

4 Choose three list words you find difficult, then make up a mnemonic for each.

Spelling Rules! Student Book 6 (ISBN 9780655092636) © Janelle Ho, Helen Pearson

5 Write a list word so that the first and last part of each sentence rhymes.

The intrepid ______________ found the thief in a booth.

The saxophonist played jazz with a lot of ______________.

The locusts caused ______________ as they ate through the paddock.

We planned a simple barbecue; the party was quite ______________.

6 Use *nuisance* as an adjective and a noun.

adjective ____

noun ____

7 Circle the malapropism in each sentence. Write the correct word in the box.

The anomalies in the rock pool waved their tentacles.	
Keep quiet and don't be such a nuance!	
This competition is only open to armchairs.	
The compendium was that the suspect couldn't be in two places at one time.	

8 Find one word or phrase in each sentence for which a list word is a synonym. Circle the word or phrase you have chosen and write the synonym in the box.

The basement was a maze of storerooms and passageways.	
Dad gave an off-the-cuff speech at his birthday dinner.	
The article was full of vocabulary that only experts could understand.	

Tip

Similes describe something by comparing it to something else using *like* or *as*.
Her hair was like silk.
Metaphors describe something by saying it *is* something else.
Her hair was black silk.

9 Write a simile and a metaphor to describe an eclipse.

simile ____

metaphor ____

Answer: b

Unit 33

An **angklong** is:

a a very long rowboat
b an Indonesian musical instrument
c an angle on the long side of a rectangle

Say Listen Look Understand Remember Practise

trek	____________
snorkel	____________
mammoth	____________
deluxe	____________
carnival	____________
rampage	____________
maestro	____________
berserk	____________
gruesome	____________
cologne	____________
abseil	____________
souvenir	____________
gourmet	____________
silhouette	____________
entrepreneur	____________

1 Fill in the silent letters.

gourme_ sil_ouette colo_ne

Tip Some words can be both nouns and verbs.
*I **spy** a fly. I didn't know he was a **spy**.*

2 Write a sentence for each meaning of these words.

trek (noun): ____________

trek (verb): ____________

snorkel (noun): ____________

snorkel (verb): ____________

3 Use a dictionary to find out where each list word comes from.

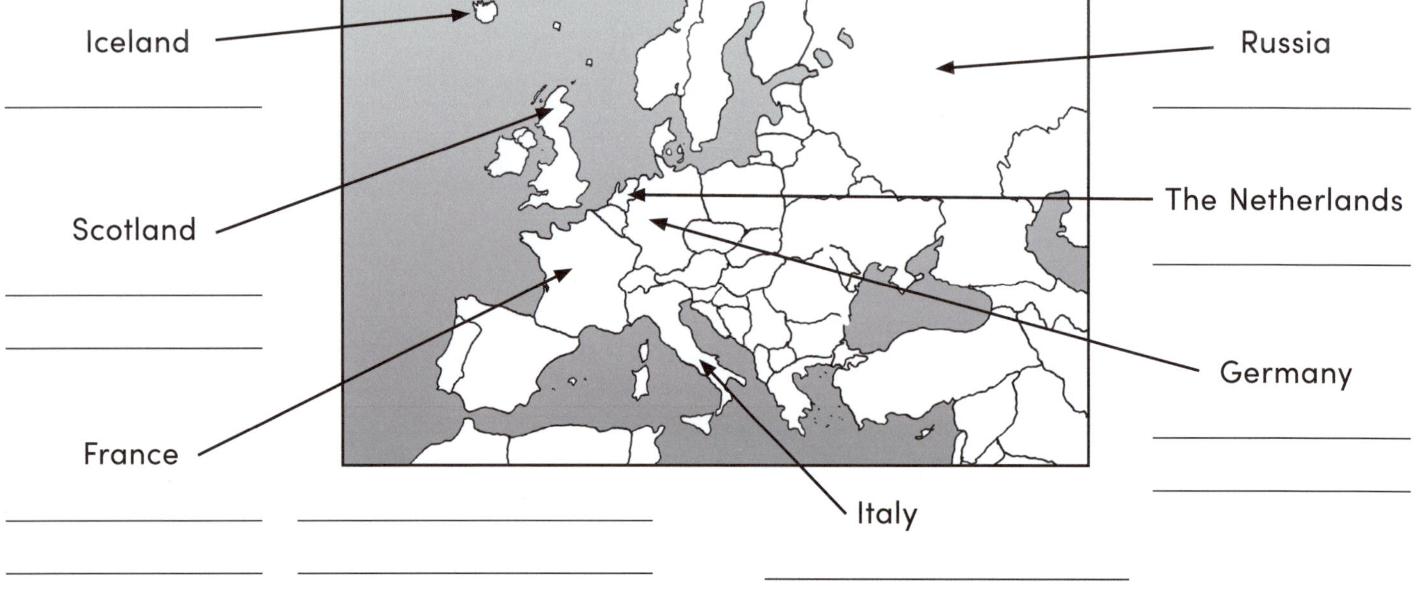

Spelling Rules! Student Book 6 (ISBN 9780655092636) © Janelle Ho, Helen Pearson

4 Use list words to complete the puzzle.

Across

2. wild and frenzied
5. perfume
6. long and difficult journey
7. tube for breathing underwater
8. of excellent taste
10. gigantic
11. business person
12. a holiday keepsake
13. destructive behaviour
14. of superior quality

Down

1. to descend using a rope
3. an outline
4. a distinguished musician
8. horrific
9. a travelling fair or sports meet

5 Write list words you might use when talking about these topics.

war ____________________

sports ____________________

people ____________________

your senses ____________________

Answer: b

Unit 34

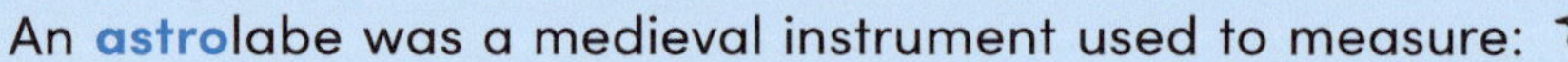

An **astro**labe was a medieval instrument used to measure:

a the altitude of the stars and planets
b how much water stars hold
c how many labradors there are in space

Say **L**isten **L**ook **U**nderstand **R**emember **P**ractise

asteroid ______
astronaut ______
astronomy ______
comet ______
galaxy ______
meteor ______
orbit ______
dimension ______
futuristic ______
chronology ______
medieval ______
terrestrial ______
archaeologist ______
palaeontology ______
Renaissance ______

1 Sort the list words according to whether they are related to time or space. Some words may fit both categories.

time: ______

space: ______

Write the word that is French in origin and means 'rebirth'.

______

Tip The prefix **astro** comes from the Greek word for *star*.

2 Use the definitions to complete the puzzle.

1.	A	S	T	E	R					
2.	A	S	T	E	R					
3.	A	S	T	R	O					
4.	A	S	T	R	O					
5.	A	S	T	R	O					

1. a structure that revolves around the sun
2. name of the symbol *
3. a space traveller
4. the study of the universe
5. a person who studies the universe

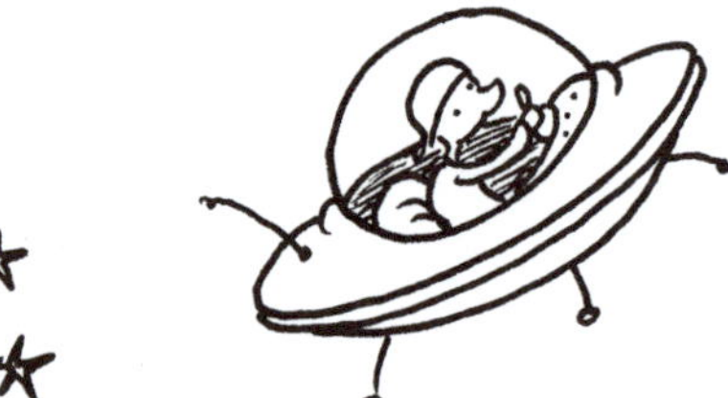

Spelling Rules! Student Book 6 (ISBN 9780655092636) © Janelle Ho, Helen Pearson

3 Use each clue to find a smaller word within a list word. Write the small word and the list word.

clue	small word	list word
a sphere	________	________
opposite of go	________	________
male adults	________	________
to have a break	________	________

Tip An **idiom** is a group of words always used in a fixed expression.

4 Write the meaning of each idiom.

out of this world ________

to work like clockwork ________

par for the course ________

a dog's breakfast ________

in the nick of time ________

know it like the back of your hand ________

5 Write the correct form of a list word to complete each sentence.

Two of the first ________ to land on the moon were Neil Armstrong and John Glenn.

Takei has had a ________ rise in the company. He's worked there for only a year and is already a manager.

A ________ is someone who studies fossils in order to discover more about extinct plants and animals. Part of the job is working out the ________ order of events so as to trace the evolution of these plants and animals.

A shape like a circle or square is two-________ because it only has length and breadth. A sphere and a cylinder have three ________ because they also have depth and can contain things.

Aliens can also be called ________ creatures. Most movies portray such creatures as frightening.

Answer: a

Unit 35 Revision

One of the longest words in the English language is **floccinaucinihilipilification**. It means:

a having hallucinations about sheep
b climbing hills repeatedly
c the act of estimating something as worthless

1 Write the word for each picture.

 ____________

 ____________

 ____________

 ____________

 ____________

 ____________

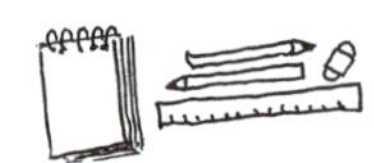 ____________

 ____________

2 Complete the table by building word families.

verb	past tense	noun	adjective	adverb
wonder				
	predicted			
		explosion		
			suspicious	
				decisively

3 Some of the vowels have been left out of these words. Add the missing vowels.

___wkw___rd	t___tion
___rch___logist	___rie
fl___rescent	baz___r
s___ven___r	f___na

4 Some of the consonants have been left out of these words. Add the missing consonants.

ex___e___	fra___ure
enviro___ent	bu___et
___eumonia	a___end
e___erve___ence	co___a___orate

5 Write a word to match each definition.

a long piece of music played by a large orchestra ____________

someone new and inexperienced ____________

able to speak many languages ____________

a false name ____________

a many-sided shape ____________

an act of betrayal ____________

pretend someone else's words are your own ____________

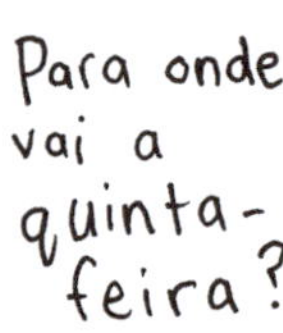

Spelling Rules! Student Book 6 (ISBN 9780655092636) © Janelle Ho, Helen Pearson

6 Each word has been written as it sounds. Rewrite it correctly.

converless	daybew	show fur	may tree ark
________	________	________	________
rithum	canserlation	missalayneeus	backteeriah
________	________	________	________

7 Add **g** or **j**.

ad__acent	avera__e	passen__er	__ustice	ur__ent
re__oice	fra__ile	challen__e	pre__udice	__ud__ement

8 Add the letters that make the **er** sound.

p__manent	v__tual	c__cular	categ__y	dist__b
j__ney	p__l	reh__se	c__tesy	b__s__k

9 Add **al**, **el** or **le**.

practic__	seri__	chort__	sequenti__	vehic__
gradu__	parall__	optic__	wrest__	skelet__

10 Circle any words in each sentence that do not make sense. Rewrite each sentence so it makes sense.

The train terminals at the next stop.

____

When I had affluence, the doctor listened to my chest with a periscope.

____

'You'd better have a good exclamation for being late,' said Boris.

____

At dinner, Doug ate an access of dessert. No wonder his digression was affected!

____

We sat on the terrain last night to watch the meter shower.

____

The confetti on the window made it hard to look at the scenario.

____

Answer: c

LIST WORDS IN UNIT ORDER

Unit 1
genre
geometry
genealogy
gyrate
indulge
grudge
judgement
jubilant
jest
juvenile
junction
hijack
prejudice
adjacent
adjoining

Unit 2
corruption
exhibition
exception
restriction
distinction
desperation
cooperation
alliteration
devastation
hallucination
deception
evolution
resolution
revolution
prescription

Unit 3
possession
obsession
extension
suspension
expansion
corrosion
invasion
exclusion
collision
persuasion
provision
admission
submission
inversion
diversion

Unit 4
flee
pursue
statue
venue
cocoa
mosquito
rodeo
eerie
simile
guarantee
refugee
committee
verandah
debut
alibi

Unit 5
government
parliament
cabinet
politician
minister
senator
representatives
governor
premier
opposition
president
election
democracy
monarchy
federal

Unit 7
synthesise
idiosyncrasy
syndrome
sympathy
symbiotic
symmetry
coherent
cohesive
coincidence
coordinate
accommodate
commotion
compensate
correlate
collaborate

Unit 8
coach
pilot
lifeguard
locksmith
optician
treasurer
choreographer
courier
tutor
sculptor
surgeon
analyst
pharmacist
athlete
paramedic

Unit 9
durability
probability
acceptability
compatibility
predictability
variability
changeability
irritability
visibility
flexibility
vulnerability
accessibility
invincibility
eligibility
susceptibility

Unit 10
environment
rainforest
pollution
greenhouse
climate
recycle
ozone
ecology
irrigation
conservation
deforestation
flora
fauna
sustainable
atmosphere

Unit 11
biology
biography
autobiography
biodegradable
microbe
zoology
zoophobia
anthropology
philanthropy
anthropomorphism
geology
geography
terrace
terrain
terrestrial

Unit 13
prior
senior
superior
exterior
posterior
deteriorate
median
alliance
valiant
pliant
ruffian
peculiar
plagiarise
matriarch
diarrhoea

Unit 14
telescope
periscope
aspect
suspect
auspicious
conspicuous
despise
despicable
spectacle
speculate
sequence
sequel
execute
prosecute
consecutive

Unit 15
wondrous
perilous
miraculous
Indigenous
cantankerous
ferocious
gregarious
rebellious
voracious
precarious
instantaneous
spontaneous
righteous
continuous
ambiguous

Unit 16
novel
novelty
novice
innovate
innovation
vocal
vocabulary
advocate
vociferous
invoke
provoke
notice
notify
annotate
reminisce

Unit 17
solution
toxic
method
experiment
acid
alkaline
temperature
evaporate
thermometer
theory
equipment
chemical
microscope
hypothesis
laboratory

Unit 19
definition
repetition
condemnation
alteration
interpretation
continuation
declaration
cancellation
inflammation
explanation
exclamation
variation
identification
notification
clarification

Unit 20
military
anniversary
solitary
documentary
contrary
crockery
confectionery
surgery
nursery
treachery
forgery
sensory
contradictory
category
exploratory

Unit 21
enclose
engorge
entangle
extricate
exhale
excavate
exorbitant
precede
prelude
precursor
procession
prologue
procrastinate
proportion
postscript

Unit 22
symphony
phonetic
microphone
cacophony
synonym
antonym
pseudonym
anonymous
empathy
telepathy
majesty
majority
magnify
magnificent
magnanimous

Unit 23
medicine
bacteria
virus
pregnant
fracture
organ
influenza
abdomen
intestine
capsule
appendix
vaccination
immunisation
pneumonia
stethoscope

Unit 25
cyclone
cynical
cyberspace
urgency
accuracy
literacy
numeracy
privacy
pregnancy
diplomacy
adequacy
delicacy
obstinacy
buoyancy
legacy

Unit 26
subconscious
sublime
submerge
subordinate
subside
substandard
subterranean
subtle
succinct
succumb
suffocate
suppose
supplement
surreptitious
suspend

Unit 27
subconscious
sublime
submerge
subordinate
subside
substandard
subterranean
subtle
succinct
succumb
suffocate
suppose
supplement
surreptitious
suspend

Unit 28
incomprehension
unmanageable
discontinued
ignorance
invisibility
irrational
immobile
immovable
noticeably
symmetrical
unintentionally
uncritically
reversible
illegibly
predestined

Unit 29
currency
exchange
pound
euro
rupiah
baht
allowance
financial
budget
discount
subsidy
purchase
expenditure
millionaire
treasury

Unit 31
ascend
descend
transcend
scenario
obscene
adolescent
fluorescent
iridescent
effervescent
miscellaneous
convalesce
scintillate
conscience
conscientious
resuscitate

Unit 32
onomatopoeia
asphalt
amateur
havoc
jargon
anemone
flummox
sleuth
nuisance
naive
pizzazz
eclipse
impromptu
labyrinth
conundrum

Unit 33
trek
snorkel
mammoth
deluxe
carnival
rampage
maestro
berserk
gruesome
cologne
abseil
souvenir
gourmet
silhouette
entrepreneur

Unit 34
asteroid
astronaut
astronomy
comet
galaxy
meteor
orbit
dimension
futuristic
chronology
medieval
terrestrial
archaeologist
palaeontology
Renaissance

List words in alphabetical order

abbreviation	Unit 26
abdomen	Unit 23
abseil	Unit 33
acceptability	Unit 9
accessibility	Unit 9
accommodate	Unit 7
accuracy	Unit 25
acid	Unit 17
adequacy	Unit 25
adjacent	Unit 1
adjoining	Unit 1
admission	Unit 3
adolescent	Unit 31
advocate	Unit 16
alibi	Unit 4
alkaline	Unit 17
alliance	Unit 13
alliteration	Unit 2
allowance	Unit 29
alteration	Unit 19
amateur	Unit 32
ambiguous	Unit 15
analyst	Unit 8
anemone	Unit 32
anniversary	Unit 20
annotate	Unit 16
anonymous	Unit 22
antonym	Unit 22
appendix	Unit 23
athlete	Unit 8
anthropology	Unit 11
anthropomorphism	Unit 11
apparatus	Unit 26
archaeologist	Unit 34
ascend	Unit 31
aspect	Unit 14
asphalt	Unit 32
assassin	Unit 26
asteroid	Unit 34
astronaut	Unit 34
astronomy	Unit 34
atmosphere	Unit 10
auspicious	Unit 14
autobiography	Unit 11
bacteria	Unit 23
baht	Unit 29
berserk	Unit 33
biodegradable	Unit 11
biography	Unit 11
biology	Unit 11
budget	Unit 29
buoyancy	Unit 25
cabinet	Unit 5
cacophony	Unit 22
cancellation	Unit 19
cantankerous	Unit 15
capsule	Unit 23
carnival	Unit 33
category	Unit 20
changeability	Unit 9
clarification	Unit 19
chemical	Unit 17
choreographer	Unit 8
chronology	Unit 34
climate	Unit 10
coach	Unit 8
cocoa	Unit 4
coherent	Unit 7
cohesive	Unit 7
coincidence	Unit 7
collaborate	Unit 7
collision	Unit 3
cologne	Unit 33
comet	Unit 34
committee	Unit 4
commotion	Unit 7
compatibility	Unit 9
compensate	Unit 7
condemnation	Unit 19
confectionery	Unit 20
contradictory	Unit 20
contrary	Unit 20
conscience	Unit 31
conscientious	Unit 31
consecutive	Unit 14
conservation	Unit 10
conspicuous	Unit 14
continuation	Unit 19
continuous	Unit 15
conundrum	Unit 32
convalesce	Unit 31
cooperation	Unit 2
coordinate	Unit 7
correlate	Unit 7
corrosion	Unit 3
corruption	Unit 2
courier	Unit 8
crockery	Unit 20
currency	Unit 29
cyberspace	Unit 25
cyclone	Unit 25
cynical	Unit 25
debut	Unit 4
deception	Unit 2
declaration	Unit 19
definition	Unit 19
deforestation	Unit 10
delicacy	Unit 25
deluxe	Unit 33
democracy	Unit 5
descend	Unit 31
desperation	Unit 2
despicable	Unit 14
despise	Unit 14
deteriorate	Unit 13
devastation	Unit 2
diarrhoea	Unit 13
dilemma	Unit 26
dimension	Unit 34
diplomacy	Unit 25
discontinued	Unit 28
discount	Unit 29
distinction	Unit 2
diversion	Unit 3
documentary	Unit 20
durability	Unit 9
eccentric	Unit 26
eclipse	Unit 32
ecology	Unit 10
eerie	Unit 4
effervescent	Unit 31
election	Unit 5
eligibility	Unit 9
empathy	Unit 22
enclose	Unit 21
engorge	Unit 21
entangle	Unit 21
entrepreneur	Unit 33
environment	Unit 10
equipment	Unit 17
etiquette	Unit 26
euro	Unit 29
evaporate	Unit 17
evolution	Unit 2
excavate	Unit 21
exception	Unit 2
exchange	Unit 29
exclamation	Unit 19
exclusion	Unit 3
execute	Unit 14
exhale	Unit 21
exhibition	Unit 2
exorbitant	Unit 21
expansion	Unit 3
expenditure	Unit 29
experiment	Unit 17
explanation	Unit 19
exploratory	Unit 20
extension	Unit 3
exterior	Unit 13
extricate	Unit 21
fauna	Unit 10
federal	Unit 5
ferocious	Unit 15
financial	Unit 29
flee	Unit 4
flexibility	Unit 9
flora	Unit 10
flummox	Unit 32
fluorescent	Unit 31
forgery	Unit 20
fracture	Unit 23
futuristic	Unit 34
galaxy	Unit 34
genealogy	Unit 1
genre	Unit 1
geography	Unit 11
geology	Unit 11
geometry	Unit 1
gimmick	Unit 26
gourmet	Unit 33
government	Unit 5
governor	Unit 5
graffiti	Unit 26
greenhouse	Unit 10
gregarious	Unit 15
grudge	Unit 1
gruesome	Unit 33
guarantee	Unit 4
gyrate	Unit 1
hallucination	Unit 2
havoc	Unit 32
hijack	Unit 1
hypothesis	Unit 17
identification	Unit 19
idiosyncrasy	Unit 7
ignorance	Unit 28
illegibly	Unit 28
immobile	Unit 28
immovable	Unit 28
immunisation	Unit 23
impromptu	Unit 32
incomprehension	Unit 28
Indigenous	Unit 15
indulge	Unit 1
inflammation	Unit 19
influenza	Unit 23
innovate	Unit 16
innovation	Unit 16
instantaneous	Unit 15
intermittent	Unit 26
interpretation	Unit 19
intestine	Unit 23
invasion	Unit 3
inversion	Unit 3
invincibility	Unit 9
invisibility	Unit 28
invoke	Unit 16
iridescent	Unit 31
irrational	Unit 28
irrigation	Unit 10
irritability	Unit 9
jargon	Unit 32
jest	Unit 1
jubilant	Unit 1
judgement	Unit 1
junction	Unit 1
juvenile	Unit 1

SPELLING RULES AND TIPS

- The general term for prefixes and suffixes is **affixes**.

- **Adding ion**

  If a word ends in **scribe**, change **scribe** to **script** before adding **ion**.

  describe → description

  If a word ends in **ceive**, change **ceive** to **cept** before adding **ion**.

  receive → reception

  If a word ends in **t**, change **t** to **ss** before adding **ion**.

  admit → admission

  If a word ends in **nd**, change **d** to **s** before adding **ion**.

  extend → extension

  If a word ends in **lve**, change **ve** to **ut** before adding **ion**.

  solve → solution

  If a word ends in **y**, change the **y** to **i** before adding **cation**.

  multiply → multiplication

  Some exceptions: *vary → variation*   *satisfy → satisfaction*

- **Adding al**

  If a noun ends in **ce**, change the **ce** to **ti** before adding **al** to make the adjective.

  confidence → confidential

  Exceptions: *office → official*   *practice → practical*

- **Adding ity**

  Words ending in **ible** and **able** are adjectives.
  These words may also add **ity** as a second suffix.
  Adding **ity** changes the adjective to a noun.

  probable → probability   *visible → visibility*

- The prefix **com-** means *with* or *together*.
  Use **com-** before **b**, **p** or **m**. *combine*
  Use **col-** before **l**. *collapse*
  Use **cor-** before **r**. *correlate*
  Use **co-** before **h** or **gn**. *cognition*
  Use **con-** in all other cases. *confuse*

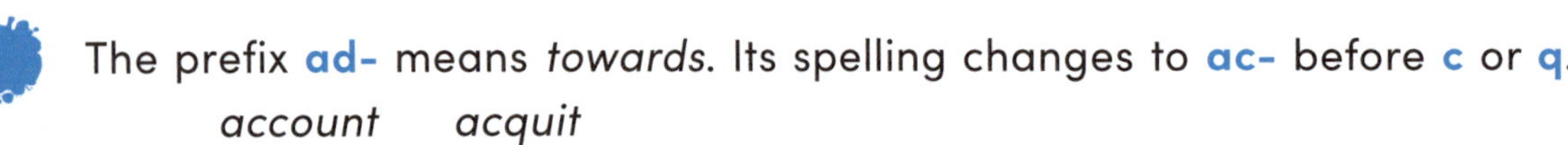

- The prefix **ad-** means *towards*. Its spelling changes to **ac-** before **c** or **q**.

  account   *acquit*

- The prefix **sub-** means *under* or *less than*. The letter **b** may change to match the beginning consonant of the base word.

  submit   *suppose*   *sufficient*   *succumb*

Spelling Rules! Student Book 6 (ISBN 9780655092636) © Janelle Ho, Helen Pearson